Scientologist!

William S. Burroughs
and the 'Weird Cult'

by David S. Wills

A Beatdom Books Publication

Published by Beatdom Books

Copyright © 2013 by David S. Wills
Cover photograph by Charles Gatewood

View the publisher's website:
www.books.beatdom.com

Printed in the United Kingdom
First Print Edition
ISBN 978-0-9569525-2-3

Contents

Introduction

Mentor to Allen Ginsberg and Jack Kerouac, William S. Burroughs is considered the wise man of the Beat Generation, a legend of the counterculture, and an inspiration to millions. His intelligence and wit are beyond reproach, and it is obvious to anyone who's ever managed to decipher his notoriously difficult books that he possesses the sharpest and most skeptical of minds. It is perhaps for these reasons that so many are surprised when they learn of his interest in Scientology, and assume that his exploration of the religion was merely a brief encounter for the purpose of producing a work of investigative journalism.

Of course, this view presupposes a complete lack of credibility on the part of the religion in question. Fifty years later, it is hard to imagine a time when Scientology may once have appealed to intellectuals or, indeed, any sane or reasonable person. With negative publicity focusing on the likes of Tom Cruise, lawsuits, celebrity centers, and stories about spaceships – not to mention high profile exposes and satires – it has become little more than tabloid fodder for those outside its ranks. It is now a laughing stock that is hard for anyone to take seriously, and I'm sure that my use of the word "religion" throughout this book will shock a number of my readers, who are more comfortable with the application of the term "cult."

For William S. Burroughs, however, Scientology offered serious gifts to humanity, a potential cure to a number of personal problems, a new avenue in literature, a weapon in the fight against systems of control, and justification for a number of his other obsessions in the realm of "fringe science." In other words, it was extremely important to him during one of the most creatively fertile periods of his life. Although he was never enamored with the Church's leadership or much of its doctrine, and in fact was required to suppress his contempt for its founder, L. Ron Hubbard, he went beyond merely being a spectator, taking courses and tests over a period of nearly a decade, before finally achieving the status of "clear" – a significant event for a member of the Church, and one that by no means all members are capable of achieving. Scientology affected his life and work from his earliest encounters with it until his final days. Despite his well-publicized fallout with the religion, he learned from it and used it in the creation of his finest literary works.

Although his literature is clearly influenced by Hubbard's ideas, and his letters during the sixties and seventies littered with references to Scientology, and despite his overt interest in it, both as an adherent and an enemy, Scientology is largely sidelined in otherwise sterling books and essays about his life and work. When Ted Morgan, in *Literary Outlaw*, refers to Scientology as a "new passion" for Burroughs in 1968, he completely overlooks the religion's influence over the past eight years of Burroughs' life, and fails to recognize its role in some of his most important books. Barry Miles, in *El Hombre Invisible*, states that Burroughs had only "tinkered around" with it until 1967 (Miles mistakenly listed Burroughs' enrollment as January, 1967, when in fact it was January, 1968), and in *Beat Hotel* claims that he was expelled from the organization in the early seventies, when in fact he was kicked out in 1969. When they come to Burroughs' time at Saint Hill, the Scientology training center in England, his biographers give very few pages over to his experiences, and fail to tie them into his life and work in a greater sense. Yet it was tremendously important. Only Douglas Kahn, in his essay "Two Sounds of the Virus," appears to have grasped the significance of Scientology on Burroughs' literary output, commenting:

> "The degree to which Burroughs adopted Hubbard's theory of recording and fused it with the virus, and the degree with which a new mythology of the space age was infused with both, was repeatedly demonstrated in his writings."

Throughout his life, Burroughs had a number of obsessions. He was interested in fringe science, and in the weird and exotic. He was also a deeply disturbed man, loaded down with dark memories, insecurities, and traumas. His books are often criticized as difficult or even inaccessible, but when you look at his life, taking into consideration his more oddball interests, they make sense. From Count Alfred Korzybski's General Semantics to Wilhelm Reich's Deadly Orgone Radiation, we see a man attracted to explanations and potential cures for his peculiar mix of problems, including childhood traumas, the death of his wife, his homosexuality, and drug use. Indeed, when one looks at Scientology, it is hard to imagine a system more appealing to a man like Burroughs.

During their stay at the Beat Hotel in Paris, the artist Brion Gysin held tremendous influence over Burroughs, and introduced him to numerous areas of interest, including the legend of Hassan ibn Sabbah. In 1959 Gysin introduced Burroughs to L. Ron Hubbard's *Dianetics*, which was the foundation of Scientology, and the effect was immediate: Scientology merged with his existing beliefs and ideas and became a part of him. It changed his views on life and literature, influencing the creation of the Cut-up Method and informing his notion of the word as a virus. Even after his public fallout with the Church, nearly a decade later, the primary notions espoused by Hubbard would remain with Burroughs forever.

Throughout the sixties, his work was heavily inspired by

Scientology. Within six months of reading *Dianetics*, Hubbard's name and his ideas were already in Burroughs' newest book, *Minutes to Go*. Another year later and he wrote *The Soft Machine*: a novel absolutely derived from Scientology. It plays a significant role in the rest of the Nova Trilogy, and was the subject of numerous essays, articles, and short stories during the course of the decade. Even in the seventies and eighties it appears in his work, inspiring the composition of *The Wild Boys* and developing his theories of space travel, which he explored in later novels. Hubbard's reactive mind and his engrams, along with other parts of Scientology, permanently entered and altered Burroughs' worldview.

For Burroughs, perhaps the most important feature of Scientology was its potential as a means of fighting the systems of control. Of course, this may seem a little ironic, given Scientology's control over its adherents, and its attempts at control elsewhere. However, for Burroughs its methods could be applied in art and in life, and he studied them seriously for many years. As he studied, his interest grew. He went through patches of distrust, seemingly wiping his hands of the religion in 1967, before being sucked in once again during an attempt to write an exposé. But through his ups and downs, Scientology was as much of an obsession as, for example, the Mayans or orgone theory.

This has been largely overlooked. It is only when Burroughs had his public fallout with the Church, taking his battle to the pages of national publications, that anyone seems interested in exploring his take on Scientology. There are various reasons for this. Given current knowledge about Scientology, it seems hard to believe that Burroughs could have been so readily sucked in, and it is desirable to portray him as a heroic crusader against the "weird cult," rather than a one-time follower. Additionally, his attacks on the Church are easier to come upon. Burroughs' articles advocating Scientology are buried away in the numerous small press publications of the sixties, and the references in his Nova Trilogy are hidden among other obscure science-fiction terminology, whereas the prevalence of anti-Scientology websites has made it easy enough to get a hold of his later works, such as *Ali's Smile/Naked Scientology*.

Regardless, in treating William S. Burroughs as a serious literary figure, it is important to avoid the trap of portraying him as we would like him to be seen. The purpose of this book, therefore, is not to celebrate or mock Scientology, but to explore its importance in the life of an American literary giant. It will demonstrate not only why Scientology was so appealing to Burroughs, but how his life made it almost inevitable that he would take to the religion with such zeal. I will show how the work of L. Ron Hubbard influenced the creation of the Cut-Up Method and became part of the Burroughsian universe. This book will follow a strictly chronological path, examining the beliefs and experiences of the young Burroughs until his first encounter with Scientology in 1959, before then looking at his decade-long relationship with the religion. I will explore the references to Scientology in his novels, which have thus far gone ignored, possibly due to their obscure nature. I will also examine the public fall-out between Burroughs and the Church and how, in spite of everything, he still held some of Hubbard's ideas to be valuable throughout the remainder of his life.

Wog:

1914-1959

William Seward Burroughs II was born to Mortimer and Laura Lee Burroughs on Pershing Avenue in St. Louis, Missouri, on February 5th, 1914. Known as the "show me state" of skeptics and entrepreneurs, Missouri's reputation was carved out by men such as his paternal grandfather, William Seward Burroughs, the inventor of the Burroughs Adding Machine. His legacy was a source of basic finance for the family, however, it did not, as Jack Kerouac and others liked to suggest, amount to a vast wealth. Despite their modest fame and financial security, they were stuck in a sort of social limbo; viewed as riff-raff by the true St. Louis elite, but nonetheless part of a wider upper class. Their finances extended to a large home in a good neighborhood and a number of servants, but they were not invited to the most prestigious parties. Burroughs later spoke with some venom of the millionaire "WASP elite," that surrounded them, and said, "nobody wanted those ratty Burroughses around."

On his mother's side he supposedly descended from Robert E. Lee, although this is a common claim for people with her Southern background. Laura's brother "Poison" Ivy was partly responsible for the invention of the field of public relations, and was hired to by the Nazis to manage Hitler's image in the United States, and by John D. Rockefeller Jr. following the 1914 Ludlow Massacre. Burroughs later reflected upon his family's history as one of capitalists warping truth and language for personal gain, and claimed that Ivy "never liked me. I *saw* too much." His lack of respect for Ivy and his profession continued throughout his life, and may have influenced his choice of the pseudonym "William Lee."

Mortimer and Laura appear to have been atheists, but Laura came from a deeply religious Southern family. To appease her parents, and likely to keep up appearances for the sake of the society of which they desperately wanted to be a part, their children (Billy had one brother, also named Mortimer) were sent to Sunday school. Young Billy had a strong distaste for hypocrisy even as a child, and was unhappy with his parents for this injustice. They forced him to go to church until his Methodist grandfather, Laura's father, died when Billy was six years old. However, throughout his life, despite a general aversion to religion, Burroughs never doubted the existence of an afterlife or of gods, and even argued with his father at a young age that some form of god must exist.

Although not religious, Laura was psychic and claimed to have intuitions about people that proved startlingly accurate and she once claimed to have foretold a car accident involving her son, Mort. She saw ghosts and used crystal balls and Ouija boards to contact the other side. Laura came across as cold, indifferent, and even cruel in the eyes of people around her, but she had a soft spot for Billy, and mothered him embarrassingly. Showing little affection towards her eldest, Mort, she had no problem telling Billy, "I worship the ground you walk on." On the other hand, Billy didn't get along well with his father, who seemed to prefer the stronger, more athletic of his two sons. He would heap praise upon Mort but forbid Billy from participating in father-son activities.

Alongside the family, there were a number of servants. The cook was an old Irish woman who awakened in Billy a life-long interest in the occult. It began with a trick called "calling the toads," which involved making a hooting sound to draw out a big fat toad from under its stone. She also taught him his first curse – called the "blinding worm." She explained that it was possible to blind a person by running some thread through a piece of stale bread and burying it in a pigsty, chanting:

> Needle in thread
> Needle in bread
> Eye in needle
> Needle in eye
> Bury the bread deep in a sty

There was also another rhyme that could protect you against the "blinding worm," should anyone else try to place this curse upon you.

Unsurprisingly, Billy began to view the world as a place of darkness and magic, and always looked back upon his childhood as a time of confusion and fear. Between his mother's premonitions and the secret curses told to him by the cook, his outlook was being quickly shaped to incorporate elements of the supernatural as though they were perfectly normal. He suffered nightmares all through childhood, and even experienced hallucinations or visions. The first was of a green reindeer, which he thought was his protector, and the other was a number of small men living inside a house that he had made out of toy blocks. Once, at five years of age, he was so overcome by a sense of hopelessness that he burst out crying, and later identified the moment as the visitation of a dark spirit.

His nanny, Mary Evans, served to further his odd view of the world. She taught him another curse, one that he remembered decades later in *The Place of Dead Roads:*

Trip and stumble
Slip and fall
Down the stairs
And hit the wall

The relationship between Billy and his nanny is a source of mystery and great importance in examining his life. He is known to have been very close with Mary Evans, and was uncontrollably distraught whenever she would leave, causing biographer Ted Morgan to speculate that she had employed the technique of sexual stimulation to pacify the child.

But despite his attachment to her, Mary was a source of tremendous darkness in Billy's life. Her boyfriend – a veterinarian, who would make the infant watch as he euthanized animals –accompanied the two of them on a trip outdoors when Billy was four years old. Despite Burroughs' nearly photographic memory, which extended back even into early childhood, this day was a blur to him and the source of much pain and misery throughout his entire life. There was some sort of conspiracy. The nanny attempted to coerce Billy into doing something with her boyfriend that Billy did not enjoy, and later threatened him with a curse, explaining that his eyes would be sucked out of his head if he spoke about what happened. He appears to have told his brother something, and shortly after his mother explained that "nursy" was going away for good. This time, Billy did not cry.

The event caused the young boy to lose faith in his family, and particularly in his mother. This was a woman who claimed to possess psychic powers. She had accurately picked out crooked businessmen from legitimate ones, and had foretold certain events, but had failed to tell that Mary was a bad person. She had not protected her four-year-old child from what was most likely sexual abuse, an event that would cause him immense trauma for the rest of his life. It may also have played a role in his dim view of women, whom he considered either evil or weak.

Young Billy was an odd child and struggled to make friends. This was likely true prior to the encounter with Mary Evans' boyfriend, but certainly it would not have made socializing any easier. Indeed, his family life made normal socializing impossible for him, as his mother mollycoddled him and his father virtually ignored him. From the earliest days of his life, people thought him weird and unpleasant. He was shunned, and retained this feeling of alienation well into adulthood. One of his classmates' parents compared him to a "sheep-killing dog," and another said that he "looks like a walking corpse:"

Billy was made to attend a different school to his brother. According to Mort, Billy's school was for "sissies." He was not happy there, retaining his sense of alienation, appearing odd in the eyes of his classmates and teachers, and furthering his sense of skepticism about the world around him, and in particular the people in charge. Yet it was here, at the John Burroughs School where Billy met Kells Elvins – a long-time friend and his first love. He was immediately taken with the strong and athletic boy, and they would play rather physical games that would arouse Billy. Although Kells was not a homosexual, and their relationship was that of friends, Billy's classmates could see his infatuation, and joked about it. "You're his slave," they said, as Billy walked around with his arms draped over Kells.

In 1927, when Billy was thirteen, he was experimenting with his chemistry set when it exploded in his hand, causing severe burns. He was taken to the hospital and given "nearly an adult dose" of morphine. Billy already knew what morphine was, as he had overheard one of the servants talking about it. He believed that it would give him "sweet dreams" and determined that it was cure the nightmares that plagued him. Years later he often commented that as a child he knew he would grow up to use opiates.

It was around this time that Billy picked up a book that would shape his life. He had long since escaped into fantasy worlds through reading science fiction and adventure stories, but the memoir of a proud criminal called Jack Black, *You Can't Win*, had a profound impact upon the disaffected youth, and was influential over his life and work as long as he lived. It introduced him to a criminal underworld that made more sense to the boy than the society in which he presently lived, and informed him about drugs. It also set young Billy to writing, and in 1929 he published his first essay, "Personal Magnetism," in the John Burroughs Review. It was a short personal story about an experience in being short-changed, in exploring the human mind, and systems of control. In it, the young boy is enchanted by an advertisement in a magazine, promising absurd spiritual and physical gifts for a mere two dollars. His tone is sardonic and bitter. In this teenager's writing, we can already see the qualities that made William S. Burroughs one of America's literary greats, as well as themes he would examine decades later, but also it's a view inside the mind of a terminally gullible and overly curious man, who, despite his intelligence, would fall for many cheap cons. In short, the essay foreshadows numerous later obsessions, including his fascination with the Church of Scientology.

Later, when looking back and attempting to explain when and why he'd decided to become a writer, Burroughs came up with a vaguely plausible explanation that points to the influence of pulp novels and adventure magazines on the impressionable child:

> "As a young child I wanted to be a writer because writers were rich and famous. They lounged around Singapore and Rangoon smoking opium in a yellow pongee silk suit. They sniffed cocaine in Mayfair and they penetrated forbidden swamps with a faithful native boy and lived in the native quarter of Tangier smoking hashish and languidly caressing a pet gazelle."

His stories from the time – of which there were many - were filled with grisly murders, hoboes, drugs, outlaws, and all sorts of stoic and oddball characters.

Shortly after publishing the essay, Billy's mother had him moved to Los Alamos, New Mexico, where the dry climate would better suit his sinus problems, to a place called the Ranch School, which aimed to make men out of spoiled rich brats. The school was fantastically expensive, but for a family with aspirations of joining the true elite, it was important to send their children to such an institution.

Billy hated his new school. He thought of it as a prison where he had no control over his own life, and the curriculum and teaching methodology were in even greater opposition to his own developing philosophies than at the John Burroughs School. He was told what to think and constantly argued with the teachers. Reading was frowned upon, and the boys were required to stay outside much of the time, where Billy was cold and miserable. He hated the director of the school, A.J. Connell, who sexually abused Billy while visiting his parents before Billy's enrollment at the Ranch School, leaving yet another scar on the young boy's mind. Connell was tough and contradictory, and Billy fought with him endlessly.

It was at the Ranch School, at only fifteen years old, that Billy first entered the world of substance abuse. He purchased a bottle of chloral hydrate from a local pharmacy and, telling the pharmacist that he was going to "commit suicide" with it, he returned to school and took an almost lethal dose. In reality, Billy was probably joking when he told the pharmacist that he wished to kill himself, and was likely exploring the effects of the drug on his mind and body. He might even have been influenced by references in the pulp novels or adventure magazines of the day. In his teens, as evidenced in his "Personal Magnetism" essay, he had become interested in alteration of the human mind – something that would continue to fascinate him for the rest of his life. It wasn't long before he snuck out on a field trip with the intention of purchasing alcohol (this was during Prohibition) and was arrested for vagrancy.

At the Ranch School, Billy became increasingly aware of, and frustrated with, his homosexuality. It was, for him, a sickness that he needed to cure. He found shame in masturbation, and was tormented by the others boys after confessing his feelings for one of his classmates. Once he put a curse on another boy after being rejected by him, and when the boy became sick Burroughs was unsurprised that it had worked. For him, curses were just a part of reality. He became depressed and withdrawn, and turned to his diary to explore his tortured soul.

Soon his mother became worried by his morbidity and had him removed from the Ranch School, citing medical problems. Billy admitted the truth to Laura: he was a homosexual. She took him to a psychiatrist, who decided that it was merely a phase, and that he would grow out of it. This was his first encounter with therapy, and the first attempt to "cure" his homosexuality. It should've been good news, but Billy was in torment. In the chaos of his hurried departure, he'd left his diary at the Ranch School. He couldn't help but imagine his classmates reading it and laughing at his confessions. But soon it arrived, forwarded on to his St. Louis address, and most likely unread. This didn't offer Billy much comfort, however, as when he opened the box and read the diary, he was filled with shame at the unabashed sentiment. He was sickened by himself, and having turned to writing to understand or cope with his troubles, he now found the act repulsive, and quit entirely for some seven years.

Despite failing to graduate from the Ranch School, Billy gained the requite high school credits at St. Louis' Taylor School, and managed to get into Harvard. Once again he found himself alienated. He was definitely not part of the hip crowd, comprised of students from fancy East Coast schools, and also cultivated a reputation, once again, as a bit of an eccentric, in no small part due to keeping a ferret and a loaded gun in his dormitory. He continued his reading, exploring but dismissing the prevalent political interests of the day (namely Communism), and greatly expanded his knowledge of literature. He was unsurprisingly enamored by Coleridge and De Quincey, who explored the effects of opiates upon the mind. However, aside from a "laughing jag" brought on by an early experience with marijuana in his dormitory, there were few drugs available to him at this time, and so he took to making his own alcohol at home.

At Harvard, he was still a virgin, and he once humiliated himself by accidently letting slip that he didn't know where babies came from. Later in life, people commented that he appeared to have never developed sexually beyond a confused sixteen year old, and that his lust for younger men stemmed from a stunted development or trauma. Although he made a few friends, he was so confused and socially inept that he was unable to make it with either gender until he was twenty, at which point he began to frequent a brothel. He was somewhat sated by knowing that he had at least done the socially acceptable thing, but still craved sex with another man. It was his final year at Harvard, in 1936, that he finally purchased a male prostitute, but contracted syphilis the very first time.

Burroughs managed to graduate, but was depressed not only by his syphilis, but by the lingering sense that he had somehow failed. Although he had earned his degree, he had not made the cut for entering a higher social stratum. His parents, however, decided to give him two hundred dollars per month as a graduation gift. This was immensely important in his life, giving him the freedom required to become a writer, rather than having to spend his time working other jobs. He set off on a "grand tour" of Europe, and decided to enroll in medical school in Vienna, where there were few prerequisites for entry to the course. As the Nazis began their push into Austria, Burroughs feared what was coming. He married a Jewish woman, Ilse Klapper, and returned to the United States to help her escape persecution.

Back in America, Burroughs was once again lost. He didn't know where to turn, first studying psychology at Columbia University in New York - where he also began a long but fairly undocumented interest in jiu-jitsu - and then he soon heard from Kells Elvins, who was still at Harvard, and decided to return there to study archeology. Throughout his life Burroughs remained interested in history and science, although always as an amateur, and ancient civilizations were always fascinating to him. Together, Kells and Billy wrote a story called "Twilight's Last Gleaming," which can be viewed as a significant landmark in Burroughs' progression as a writer. It is possibly the first example of a "routine" – the name he later used to describe comedic scenes that he acted out or wrote down – and introduced the character of Dr. Benway, who appears in many other Burroughs texts. Elvins' dark humor influenced Burroughs, and their story features the same cruel wit as much of Burroughs' later work, viciously satirizing societal norms of the day. The piece was dark and "screwy," in the words of the editors at *Esquire*, who declined to publish it. Burroughs had broken a long stretch without writing, and had made a great leap towards becoming William S. Burroughs, man of letters, but this rejection only served to put him off writing for another six years.

Although "Twilight's Last Gleaming" shows Burroughs writing in a similar fashion and on a similar topic to what he would produce as a professional author, nearly twenty years later, there were elements that were not yet in place. One of the key themes to his work, and an interest that dominated much of his life, was that of the *word*. In August, 1939, having recently read Alfred Korzybski's *Science and Sanity*, in which Korzybski posited his theory of General Semantics, Burroughs travelled to Chicago for a week-long series of lectures by his new hero. Korzybski claimed that there was a fundamental problem with language – that words didn't relate to the facts they were supposed to represent. For Burroughs, this was a major discovery. Korzybski also stated that humans were working upon a flawed system of reasoning that prevented them from seeing the world with any accuracy. They tended to see things in terms of black and white, right and wrong, without acknowledging the shades of grey or areas of moral ambiguity. Life was complicated, and hence there grew a disconnect between thought and reality. Of course, people thought in terms of words, which was further proof of this tyranny. Korzybski recommended thinking in pictures, which Burroughs attempted. All of these ideas became incorporated into Burroughs' personal philosophies and would remain with him throughout his life.

In Chicago, Burroughs also visited the Egyptology department at the University of Chicago, as his interest in archeology shifted to incorporate a growing interest in mind control through language. Thanks to Korzybski, he was beginning to consider pictorial systems of communication as a key to resisting control. During the visit, he could hear a voice in his head screaming, "YOU DON'T BELONG HERE!" and he felt as though he was partially possessed. He later connected this realization to his proximity to Egyptian hieroglyphics, and speculated that the spirit possessing him recognized their potential for combatting its method of control.

Soon Burroughs moved to New York, enrolled once again at Columbia, and met a man called Jack Anderson, with whom he fell quickly in love. The feeling, however, was not mutual, and Anderson prostituted himself to both men and women. Burroughs, in a pattern repeated throughout his life, could not hide his feelings and thus left himself open to hurt. He moved into the same building as Anderson, and sat next door, listening as the man he loved brought home countless women. When they were together, Anderson would insult Burroughs – most likely as a means of covering his own insecurities.

It was because of this relationship that Burroughs took his next foray into the world of psychotherapy, following on from his earlier attempts to alter his sexuality. This time it was Freudian analysis with Dr. Herbert Wiggers, and he felt an immediate sense of relief simply by unburdening himself. By telling the doctor what was happening with Jack, Burroughs was able to understand what he was doing, and began to make progress. However, by this stage he was a deeply troubled man and, no matter how much he wanted it, there was to be no quick fix for his blend of troubles. One day he was walking by a pawn-shop window when he saw a pair of poultry shears. After buying them, he took the shears home and sat in front of his mirror, and then, thinking of Anderson, cut off the end joint of the little finger on his left hand. Burroughs later connected this event to the incident with his nurse and her boyfriend. He was once again scared and confused, although this time he was not ashamed – he had done something he didn't understand, but he was sure it was the right thing to do.

This time, however, he was institutionalized. He took his finger to Dr. Wiggers, who insisted upon taking Burroughs to the Bellevue mental hospital, but Burroughs refused. In the end, Wiggers tricked him by telling him that he would simply go to have his finger stitched up. Just like with his nurse, and later with

A.J. Connell, he had been betrayed. Burroughs spent a month in psychiatric care, under hypno- and narcotherapy, where he first began to experience the routines that would later dominate his life and writing. In these routines he would become different characters and act out bizarre stories, for example as a redneck farmer or a Chinese peasant.

Soon he was released into his parents' guardianship, working as the deliveryman for their landscaping business. They made him continue to see therapists in order to receive his allowance, but Burroughs had soured considerably on the idea of therapy, and didn't particularly like the company of the man to whom his parents sent him. Jack Anderson came to visit him, and together they drunkenly crashed a car, landing Burroughs again in hospital. Desperately searching for something, he decided to serve his country by joining the navy, but was laughed out of the recruitment office – ever since childhood he'd been feeble and sickly. The doctor said, "He is nearsighted and flat-footed. Put down that he is a poor physical specimen." He tried numerous times to join the army and the air force, but he wasn't accepted. He was feeling more alienated than ever.

When America joined the war, Burroughs was finally enlisted. Of course, he had never wanted to be in active service. He thought of himself more as an officer, or perhaps a daring pilot. Again he was desperate to be a part of a higher class, and to gain recognition. He was miserable during his short stint at Jefferson Barracks but, fortunately for him, his mother came to the rescue by calling in a favor and drew attention to his now documented history of mental instability. During the evaluation for his discharge, he began to wonder if there wasn't something fundamentally wrong with him, some deep psychological scar.

After his discharge, Burroughs moved back to Chicago and found a therapist that he stuck with for eight whole months. This period marked the first time in his life that he ceased attempting to join a higher level of society, and sought a life more in tune with that which he'd fantasized about after reading Jack Black's *You Can't Win*. He sought out lowlifes and criminals, and took a job as an exterminator. Burroughs was attempting to build a persona as a criminal, and hatched ridiculous plots involving armed robbery. Here, he also befriended two fellow Missourians, Lucian Carr and David Kammerer. Carr was a precocious seventeen year old and Kammerer was three years older than Burroughs, at thirty-one. Kammerer was infatuated with Carr, an obsession that Burroughs knew would end badly.

Soon Carr enrolled at Columbia, and Kammerer followed him shortly after. Burroughs, who liked and respected Kammerer, followed in 1943. It was Carr that introduced Burroughs to the young Allen Ginsberg and Jack Kerouac, and almost immediately Burroughs - the damaged, fragile, confused, and alienated man – became a mentor. He was, after all, almost ten years older, better read, Harvard-educated, and had travelled around Europe. To Ginsberg, Burroughs was experienced and knowledgeable, and he later quipped, "We were like ambassadors to the Chinese emperor." He could quote Shakespeare in conversation and spoke with a cutting wit about a range of topics. He would teach them about Korzybski and suggest reading lists containing the classics, although at the time he was immersed in Raymond Chandler and Dashiell Hammett. He gave Kerouac a copy of Oswald Spengler's *Decline of the West*, and told him, "Edify your mind, my boy, with the grand actuality of the fact." Carr, Kerouac, and Ginsberg began to seek out Burroughs' opinion and Burroughs was more than happy to play the role of the wise elder. He was still an eccentric, but was no longer alienated and rejected by the people around him. The Beat Generation was coming together and he was at the very center of it.

With Kerouac and Ginsberg, Burroughs continued to act out his routines. Together they would play roles, more or less improvising scenes that were comedic and absurd. Burroughs often played female characters, and lost himself entirely in the moment. He would debate seriously with the others on literary and philosophical matters, although he began to tire of philosophizing. In particular he grew weary of Carr's constant postulating. In private, Burroughs was moving towards a simpler view, based upon Korzybski and Spengler, and centering on what he considered "facts." With Kerouac, Burroughs argued against Thomas Wolfe's style of prose. Kerouac idolized Wolfe and was moving towards a more confessional voice, whereas Burroughs, who was still scarred from the diary incident at Los Alamos, disagreed entirely. Besides, his present interest lay in a more hardboiled approach to narrative.

When Lucian Carr stabbed David Kammerer to death and rolled his body into the icy waters of the Hudson River on August 13th, 1944, he went straight to Burroughs for advice. Playing his role remarkably calm, Burroughs simply said, "So this is how Dave Kammerer ends," and flushed a bloodied packet of cigarettes down his toilet. He advised Carr to turn himself in and plead self-defense. Kammerer had, after all, followed him around America for years, pestering him without subtlety. Instead, Carr went to Kerouac, who helped him hide the remaining evidence – a pair of glasses and a knife.

When Carr eventually turned himself into the police and pled self-defense, as Burroughs had suggested, Burroughs and Kerouac were both arrested as accessories for having failed to report a murder and having assisted in disposing of evidence. In his mind, though, Burroughs was arrested for refusing to be a stool pigeon, which was absolutely outside the code of people like those in *You Can't Win*, and therefore outside his own code. Fortunately, his father bailed him out. This was a recurring pattern throughout his life – his parents would simply clean up after their disgraced son, and then act as though nothing had ever happened.

For Burroughs, the Carr case was another example of Korzybski's notion that Aristotelian thinking is flawed. The law wanted simple answers and worked on basic ideas, but reality was far more complicated than that. There was little connection between the justice system and reality. Yes, Carr had killed Kammerer, but so many angles were ignored in the effort to achieve so-called justice, such as a desire he perceived in Kammerer to be killed by the object of his affection. The whole thing seemed absurd, and helped push Burroughs further into his underworld fantasies, his distrust of words and control systems, and finally, it was a push to move him back into writing. The following year, in yet another collaborative literary effort, he wrote *And the Hippos Were Boiled in their Tanks* with Jack Kerouac. A novel about the Carr murder, the book shows the influence of Chandler and Hammett on Burroughs at this time. However, despite progressing a little further as a writer, it was yet again a false start and the piles of rejection slips caused him to take another hiatus from writing.

The Carr-Kammerer incident only temporarily broke up the group of friends, and soon Burroughs was back in New York with Kerouac and Ginsberg still eager to learn from their mentor. Burroughs had continued to undergo psychoanalysis, first with Dr. Paul Ferden, who dubbed Burroughs a "gangsterling" because of his preoccupation with the criminal underworld, and later with Dr. Lewis Wolberg, whose techniques helped Burroughs uncover a number of eccentric characters that he developed as routines. After so much therapy, Burroughs believed that he was so familiar with the techniques that he could practice them upon his friends, who held such respect for him that they both agreed. For several months, they each spent an hour a day undergoing analysis, with Ginsberg confessing his own homosexuality and Kerouac exploring issues with his mother and father.

Soon Ginsberg was kicked out of Columbia and, like Kerouac, joined the merchant marine. This was the middle of 1945 and Burroughs was feeling ashamed once again at having failed to serve his country, particularly in the light of his friends' departures, and he made another attempt to enlist. But by the time his papers came through, "Little Boy" and "Big Boy" had been dropped over the Japanese cities of Hiroshima and Nagasaki, ending nearly a quarter of a million human lives and bringing the war to an end. Burroughs was always horrified by the bombings, viewing them as the greatest dividing moment in human history. He hated the Missouri-born president who'd authorized the use of the bomb, too. Afterwards, he always maintained a strong sense of nostalgia for life before the bombings. America was changed, and he was a part of it. He felt it was no coincidence that he had gone to school in Los Alamos, where the atomic bomb was developed. He had a connection. He was a "litmus person" and couldn't help but feel his life was somehow tied to this most atrocious of acts, which brought doom and evil to the world. It was the end of civilization as Spengler had predicted.

In early 1946, he met Phil White and the career criminal Herbert Huncke, who, despite initially taking Burroughs for a cop, became close friends and business acquaintances. Burroughs had been desperate to enter the criminal underworld and here it was. He bought a tommy gun and sixteen boxes of morphine Syrettes through a friend of Jack Anderson's and sold the Syrettes on to Huncke and White, who had developed morphine habits at sea. Shortly after, Burroughs took one of the Syrettes himself. It was partly to include himself in this newfound society of criminal-types, partly a continuation of the experiment he began with the chloral hydrate at Los Alamos, and partly an extension of the reading he had done in the past few years by people like Thomas De Quincey, viewing himself again as an amateur scientist.

Burroughs enjoyed his first experiment with junk, even though it involved a nasty hallucination of a human skull, and when White came back to purchase more, he was surprised to see that Burroughs had set aside two boxes for himself. He advised his new friend against it: "It's bad stuff. The worst thing that can happen to a man." Pretty soon it was Burroughs who was buying from White, and soon he learned how to get opiates on prescription from certain doctors. They hung out together and White taught Burroughs how to inject the stuff.

By this time, Burroughs was living with Joan Vollmer and her young daughter, Julie. Vollmer had been a part of Burroughs' social circle for some time, and it had been her apartment in which many of the marathon conversations that epitomized the early Beat scene took place. She was sexually experienced and treated men like men treated women, famously rating their abilities as "cocksmen" and teaching Jack Kerouac's girlfriend, Edie Parker, how to sexually please her man. She was intelligent, too, and Ginsberg and Kerouac had long tried to set her up with Burroughs. Amazingly, despite his homosexuality and general disrespect for women, Burroughs and Vollmer hit it off. Mostly it was an intellectual relationship, but Vollmer thought

Burroughs ranked highly as a sexual partner, telling him, "You make love like a pimp." Burroughs considered her the smartest member of their group because of the way she thought. Her mind went places that the likes of Ginsberg's didn't. She introduced Burroughs to Mayan studies ("my Old lady looking up from the Mayan codices") and telepathy, which remained long-term interests of his. They would play games to test their telepathic abilities, trying to project images into the other's head for them to draw. Later they would continue this game in Mexico City, and shocked visitors with their accuracy.

Joan was always high on Bennies and Burroughs was constantly seeking out morphine, while delving further and further into the underworld. The scene was getting pretty dangerous. In particular, Huncke's thievery was putting everyone in jeopardy, as he stashed his loot in Vollmer's apartment. Then in April Phil White convinced Burroughs to go even further in his pursuit of drugs, and forge a doctor's signature, which landed him briefly in jail, where he went through withdrawal. His parents had to bail him out again, and the shock of finding that their son was a drug addict was greater than when they came to get him after the Kammerer murder.

Out of jail, Burroughs financed his habit by selling heroin and stealing from drunks on the subway with Phil White. One time a drunk woke up and turned violent, and Burroughs had to kick him. On another occasion he leant his gun to White, who used it to shoot a man, and they had to break the gun apart and hide it across the city. Burroughs was getting into more and more trouble, but luckily – as it turned out – his case came up for the forged prescription, and the judge gave an unusual verdict: "Young man, I'm going to inflict a terrible punishment on you. I'm going to send you home to St. Louis for the summer."

Once again Burroughs found himself at home with his parents. Back in St. Louis, he met up with Kells Elvins and decided to become a farmer. He bought land in Texas, near the border, and became convinced that he would get rich by selling grapefruit – a good example of his sometimes hopeless optimism. Of course, largely unchanged by the turn of events, he also planned to grow marijuana and opium poppies. But at least he was away from the New York scene, and his parents were more than relieved by this apparently remarkable change in direction.

In Texas he was in business with Elvins, and once they crossed the border to take a life-prolonging serum that was illegal in the United States. It was called the Bogomoletz serum and the Russian doctor who invented it used crude advertisements that easily lured in the highly suggestible Burroughs. He claimed that it would allow a man to live his natural life span – which was apparently one hundred and twenty-five years. Instead, Burroughs' arm swelled up badly and when he died in 1997, he was only eighty-three years old – considerably short of Bogomoletz's promise. However, despite quickly realizing that the scheme was fraudulent, he never did learn to stop believing incredible claims and bizarre promises.

Back in New York, the scene had turned ugly. Huncke's behavior was getting people in trouble, and Vollmer was soon locked up in Bellevue, where Burroughs had found himself incarcerated years before. He raced back to rescue her, and brought her down to Texas. On the way, he got Vollmer pregnant and she soon started referring to herself as his wife.

It was in Texas that Burroughs got into his next pseudo-scientific obsession. He read Wilhelm Reich's book, *The Cancer Biopathy*, in 1949, and it fitted nicely with his own views, based upon his life experiences. Reich claimed that illness was connected to social controls, and that cancer was caused by sexual repression. For a man as accustomed to alienation and suffering as Burroughs, this was an appealing idea, and he determined that his problems were the result of an intolerant society. He was also interested in Reich's interpretation of drug addiction, which again was society's fault, and excused a number of bad behaviors on the part of the addict. Throughout his life, Burroughs sought out cures, explanations, and excuses for the things that hurt him, and was often blind to their flaws or inconsistencies, of which Reichianism had many.

Having turned his back on psychiatry, he wrote to Ginsberg: "These jerks [psychiatrists] feel that anyone who is with it at all belongs in a nuthouse... I think you would do better with the Reichians who sound a good deal more hip." To Kerouac, he wrote that Reich was "the only man in the analysis line who is *on that beam*" and referred to Reich as "a fucking genius." This turn was hardly surprising, as Burroughs had run through a stream of psychiatrists in an attempt to cure his homosexuality, the lingering darkness over his childhood, his drug abuse, and the countless other problems in his life. He obviously still felt pain over having been tricked into Bellevue, and then having Joan locked up there, too.

One area of Reichianism with which Burroughs became associated, thanks largely to a description in Kerouac's *On the Road*, was that of orgone energy. Reich developed the idea of a positive form of energy, or life-force, that was present in all living things. It was also considered the opposite of bad energy – which, to Burroughs, meant nuclear material. Blocking this positive energy was, according to Reich, the cause of many of history's most awful events, and so he developed the Orgone Energy Accumulator to harness positive energy for a person to absorb. This is the box that Kerouac described after Burroughs built his own version of it on one of the Texas farms (although Kerouac erroneously placed it in New Orleans). It was 1947 when Burroughs built his first box, which was the same year that the Food and Drug Administration began its investigation into Reich, eventually determining in 1954 that the box was unfit for the public. But Burroughs was convinced of their benefits, and built several of them over his lifetime, spending around twenty minutes at a time absorbing the energy, or at least developing a tingling sensation over his body. More than once he reported experiencing orgasms from the build-up of orgones, which to him was irrefutable proof of Reich's genius.

Reichiansm was a natural step for Burroughs, and even after Reich was discredited, humiliated, imprisoned, and descended into madness, his discoveries remained facts in Burroughs' mind. In a letter to Ginsberg, Burroughs claims that Reich's flaws were "not a factor I consider of much weight," and that "his social and political theories... bore me" but "What interests me is his factual discoveries." His views appear throughout Burroughs' work – with orgones making several explicit appearances in *Naked Lunch* - and he would frequently defend the idea of orgones and societal repression as the cause of disease, even though he did eventually come to view Reich as a crackpot and a "goddamn fool" who brought about his own downfall. The whole experience closely mirrors Burroughs' later encounter with Scientology and L. Ron Hubbard.

Burroughs' experiences as a farmer were not overwhelmingly positive, and he felt the reaching hands of the government encroaching upon his life once again, even as he followed the frontier to its limits – the Mexican border. He was being told what to grow and who to hire, and he was arrested yet again, this time for fornicating by the roadside. Consequently, he began selling his property and moved to New Orleans, where he developed another bad junk habit. Soon he was arrested for possession, and began preparing to leave the United States, imagining that no country on earth could be as oppressive (and therefore, by Reichian logic, unhealthy) as his own.

Around this time, Burroughs' personal philosophies were undergoing a period of rapid development, and in his letters to Kerouac and Ginsberg, we can see him developing what he called "factualism":

> "Myself I am about to annunciate a philosophy called 'factualism.' All arguments, all nonsensical considerations as to what people 'should do,' are irrelevant. Ultimately there is only fact on all levels, and the more one argues, verbalizes, moralizes the less he will see and feel of fact. Needless to say, I will not write any formal statement on the subject. Talk is incompatible with factualism."

He had earlier expressed interest in "facts" (although obviously from his obsessions we can see that the term proved somewhat subjective) and the word appears frequently throughout his correspondence. He considered himself a man of science, and as such facts, rather than beliefs, were of absolute importance. However, in reality, what he was doing was constantly focusing on one set of views and ignoring or mocking others – clearly believing in an idea and determining that it's a "fact" because he believed it.

Six months later, Burroughs wrote Ginsberg again. Ginsberg had experienced visions of William Blake the previous summer, and his analyst had told him, "your mystical experiences are just hallucinations." Burroughs recommended Korzybski's theory of General Semantics, tying the perceived failures of psychiatry to the misuse of language:

> "Did he say in *terms of fact* what an hallucination is? No – because *he does not know*. No one knows. He is just throwing around verbiage. Frankly I was (and am) dubious of your mystical experiences because of their *vague character*. I am suspicious of "universal forces" etc. Naturally they exist, but we can only attain knowledge of such matters by concrete examples and operations. Take the question of time. Did you know that telepathy is independent of time as it is of space? (Space and time are, of course, inseparable.) Therefore everything that has ever or ever will be thought is *now* available to *all* minds… Past and Future are purely arbitrary concepts."

It is interesting that Burroughs is so determined that "we can only attain knowledge… by concrete examples and operations" and yet almost in the same breath he talks about telepathy with the utmost certainty of its existence. It should also be noted that during his time in Texas Burroughs continued his reading on the subject of the Mayans and their supposedly mind-controlling calendar system. Here is a man who believes in curses, mind control, and orgones criticizing someone for claiming that a mystical experience could be a mere hallucination.

During his time in Texas and Louisiana, Burroughs' correspondence is, aside from talk of Reich and Korzybski, very preoccupied with politics, which is something that he appeared earlier to ignore. His letters show an angry, paranoid, contradictory, and staunch conservative, raving against all forms of government control. He rants against Communists, Socialists, Fascists, and "Liberal jerks" with passionate vitriol (although these all appear to be vague forces between which he cannot differentiate). He chastises Ginsberg, in particular, for his left-leaning views, whilst complaining about the influence of the U.S. government on his farming enterprise.

In 1949, because of his hatred for the U.S. government and in his desire to escape from its laws, Burroughs fled to Mexico City. His letters show that he viewed Mexico as a land of freedom, and extension of the frontier, in stark contrast to the United States. He furthered his paranoid political views with claims that the U.S. was becoming a "Socialistic police state" and talks about "being molested by some insolent cop swollen with unwarranted authority bestowed upon him by our stupid and hysterical law-making bodies." He sounds particularly confusing and paranoid as he tirades against Ginsberg's desire to become a labor lawyer, claiming some vast conspiracy to destroy America, in line with psychiatrists and bureaucrats, always wary of a totalitarian state. In several letters he compares liberalism to cancer, at a time when Reich's *The Cancer Biopathy* was firmly in his mind, and suggests once more that reading Korzybski would help Ginsberg cure himself of his liberal mind.

He appears increasingly defensive about his other views, too. He ties into his arguments with Ginsberg the notion of telepathy, which his "personal experiments and experiences" prove to be a reality, and says, "I am concerned with *facts* on all levels of experience." Yet at the same time he is complaining about Ginsberg being too concerned with "non-supersensual reality" and "palpable objects." He angrily references experiments with orgones and his homemade accumulator, and says, "so-called Scientists... refuse to even investigate his [Reich's] findings," despite several years of investigations into Reich's invention by the Food and Drug Administration. By mid-1950, Burroughs sounds like another paranoid right-wing nut, talking himself into corners with mad theories and silly rhetoric.

In Mexico City, Burroughs' drug use continued, and Joan grew frustrated. Bill was boring on heroin. But Joan was hardly any better, as she was still hooked on Benzedrine, and the pair of them were visibly ravaged by the abuse they visited upon themselves. When Kells Elvins visited with his wife, Marianne, they were shocked to see Joan looking gaunt and vacant, and Burroughs looking half-dead. Their visit, however, was important as once again it was Elvins who encouraged Burroughs to start writing. Burroughs had been unproductive since his brief collaboration with Kerouac, broken only by an aborted attempt at sketching the reality of junk-sickness in Louisiana. Elvins told his friend to simply document his experiences as a junky, and he did. Burroughs wrote down his experiences exactly as they had happened, and by Christmas he had finished an early draft of what would become *Junky*.[1]

When Burroughs sent the book to Ginsberg, his friend claimed it was a justification of addiction, which deeply offended Burroughs. He said, "As a matter of fact the book is the only accurate account I ever read of the real horror of junk." Still, having kicked once again, and seemingly having come to the conclusion that Mexico was a little less than perfect, their correspondence is more civil than before. Burroughs' arguments are more logical and his preoccupation with U.S. politics has dissipated. At this point, Ginsberg was out of analysis and trying to go straight in every sense, and Burroughs riled at the thought of trying to cure homosexuality. It was in his mind a handicap, but not something that could be fixed. However, he doles out advice to his younger friend with wisdom and reason that were severely lacking during his earlier paranoid days: "I am acquainted with the drawbacks of being queer. More acquainted than you... the point is not how dissatisfied you are with being queer. The point is do you get everything you want in the way of sex from a

---

1 When originally published, the book was called *Junkie*, but Burroughs always maintained it should have been *Junky*, and from 1976 onwards, his version became the accepted title.

woman?" Indeed, Burroughs was familiar with this situation. He had been having sex with women for years, but still preferred the company of men. In the following letter, he compares sex with women to eating tortillas, while sex with men is like having steak. Joan, evidently possessing a sense of humor about the situation, read and annotated the letter: "Around the 20th of the month, things get a bit tight and he lives on tortillas."

During 1950-1951, Burroughs was enrolled on the G.I. Bill at Mexico City College. The exact nature of his studies is unknown, but he wrote to Ginsberg to say that he was "learning to speak Mayan and taking a course in the Codices." Burroughs later wrote about studying "Mexican archaeology," which would most likely indicate Aztec rather than Mayan, but throughout his work Burroughs commonly confuses the two civilizations, suggesting that his studies may have been somewhat half-hearted. Records indicate, though, that Burroughs was enrolled for roughly eighteen months on four courses, including – as he stated – the Mayan language, and also anthropology. He withdrew from all of these courses in July, 1951 for what one could consider a field trip…

In mid-1951, Burroughs took off for South America with Adelbert Lewis Marker - a man sixteen years younger than him - leaving Joan in Mexico City. He was in pursuit of sex and drugs, having read about various places and substances in magazines. This harkens back to his first published writing, "Personal Magnetism," showing that despite having grown up and seen some of the world, Burroughs was no less apt to believe whatever he read in a magazine. He was excitable and gullible. The first place they visited was a sad little nightclub that Burroughs had read was legendary, and then they moved on in search of yagé, which would become the chief focus of the trip, and an obsession of his over the next few years. How Burroughs came to be so obsessed with yagé is a mystery. Ginsberg later speculated that he had heard about it "in some crime magazine or National Geographic or New York Enquirer or some goofy tabloid newspaper," but at the time there was very little information about the drug anywhere. Western science knew little about it, and it's unlikely that National Geographic or any other publication would've been aware of its existence. Oliver Harris, in his introduction to *The Yagé Letters Redux*, speculates that Burroughs may have read Richard Spruce's *Notes of a Botanist on the Amazon and Andes* (1908) and Louis Lewin's *Phantasica* (1924), both of which mention the drug.

The trip was depressing for both of them. Burroughs financed it in exchange for a promise from his young companion to have sex twice a week, and yet he constantly pushed for more, and opened himself up again to be rejected and abused by the object of his affection. Still, he felt sorry for Marker, of whom he later said, "He is such a child… he doesn't realize what he is involved in. Like the pity I felt for my severed finger, as if it was innocent victim of violent, unpredictable forces. Sometimes he looks hurt and puzzled, by the warped intensity of my emotions." In addition to their relationship, the quest for yagé was also a failure. Although Burroughs had somehow obtained directions deep into the Ecuadorian jungle to meet with a mad scientist called Dr. Fuller, they ultimately failed in their attempt to find the drug and left, bitterly disappointed.

Burroughs was in bad shape when he and Marker returned to Mexico City in September. It might have been the failure of his explorations, or the constant rejection from Marker, or returning to the drudgery of family life, particularly now that Joan was in the worst state of her life. Allen Ginsberg and Lucian Carr had visited her and were shocked by her deterioration. She was drinking heavily, and claimed to have an incurable blood disease that she said would soon kill her.

Alas, it was not the drink, drugs, or any disease that killed her, but instead her husband, William S. Burroughs. In what became the best known event in his life, something that would change him forever and set him on the path to being the famous writer he became, he shot Joan dead in an horrific accident on September 6th, 1951. That day had begun badly. Burroughs took a pocket knife out to be sharpened, and was so overcome with a sense of sadness that he began crying uncontrollably in the street, and could hardly breathe. He returned home and drank.

He needed money and had arranged to sell a gun that he didn't much care for to a friend of John Healey, owner of an expat bar that Burroughs frequented, called the Bounty. They met in Healey's apartment – Joan and Bill, Lewis Marker, John Healey, and another man named Eddie Woods, a regular at the Bounty.

There are slight discrepancies between the differing accounts, but the overall picture is the same: There were only the five of them in the room, and everyone was drunk. It was Burroughs who made the suggestion. In his words, "I guess it's about time for our William Tell act." He was sitting about six to ten feet away from Joan, who willingly placed a high-ball glass on her head and stood, side-on. Burroughs fired and Joan fell to the ground, the glass landing on the ground without breaking. Marker and Woods fled the scene, going into hiding until called by Burroughs' lawyer. Burroughs was left kneeling over Joan, sobbing and crying, "Talk to me, talk to me," in disbelief at what had happened.

Later, Burroughs was never able to explain why he had done what he had done. "Something took over," he said. His marksmanship was legendary and, coupled with hours of heavy drinking, probably explains why no one said anything to stop him from firing. When Allen Ginsberg read about the shooting in a newspaper in Texas, on the way back from his trip to Mexico, he thought about Joan's attitude. She seemed, to him and Carr, to have a death wish. He wondered to what extent she had pushed her husband into shooting her. Burroughs always accepted the blame for what he had done, but also wondered if she had used the same telepathic communication to provoke him as she had used in their drawing game. Additionally, Burroughs believed that he had been given prior warning of the event. That afternoon, when overcome with emotion on the way to get his knife sharpened, he had failed to heed the sign of impending darkness.

It is impossible to overstate the importance of this event in Burroughs' life. The rest of it was spent trying to understand and atone for what happened. Every day he was reminded of what he had done. He constantly searched for a way to change history, and to cure what it was inside himself that had caused him to kill her. In the frequently cited introduction to *Queer*, published in 1985, he addressed the issue:

> "I am forced to the appalling conclusion that I would never have become a writer but for Joan's death, and to a realization of the extent to which this event as motivated and formulated my writing. I live with the constant threat of possession, and a constant need to escape from possession, from Control. So the death of Joan brought me in contact with the invader, the Ugly Spirit, and maneuvered me into a lifelong struggle, in which I have no choice but to write my way out."

Although this might sound like a cop-out, a way of both admitting and denying responsibility for a terrible accident, it was something of which Burroughs was convinced. A lot of people tend to overlook just how literally the above statement was intended to be taken. The "Ugly Spirit" of which he speaks, and the notion of "possession," is something of which Burroughs was absolutely certain. He had lived with this idea since childhood – as a part of the fear and darkness that permeated his early life, and was strongly linked to the incident with his nanny, Mary. After Joan's death, his life can be viewed as a struggle to deal with an actual demon that lived inside him. And if he was overtaken by a spirit that allowed him to kill his wife, it was still his fault; he had lost the battle and was still to blame.

It is interesting that Burroughs so explicitly linked possession and control here, as control is something that he had fought since childhood, and became an overriding theme of most of his writing. From arguing with his father to debating his teachers, from questioning the nature of language to his escape from the United States because of repressive laws, he was always attempting to beat the systems of control in his life. Possession by a demon was just the next form of control he had to battle, and this one involved a life devoted to writing.

Thankfully for Burroughs, he was spared any legal punishment by the fact that he killed Joan in Mexico. His lawyer, Bernabé Jurado, was a master of bribery and deceit, and concocted a story that the witnesses, Marker and Woods, were happy to corroborate. This involved less drinking, coupled with an accidental discharge during the sale of a weapon, and $300 to bribe a ballistics expert. He spent a total of thirteen days in jail, a record for his lawyer, who used Burroughs as a poster-boy for his criminal defense services.

Burroughs had once again shamed and shocked his family. This time his father did not come to bail him out, but instead sent William's brother, Mort. Mort held a huge amount of resentment for William's freedom, as he had been tied down with responsibilities to the family. But, for the first time, Mort dropped his guard and cried, and the two brothers shared their feelings with each other. Burroughs felt a great sense of loss for his childhood, and shame for having put his family through so much. Mort, who was drunk, comforted William. Nonetheless, when he got home he told his wife that his brother was insane.

Mort arranged for William and Joan's son, Billy, to be sent to St. Louis to live with Mortimer and Laura, but then Joan's parents arrived to claim Joan's daughter, Julie, from her previous marriage. They wanted to take Billy, too, but Burroughs told them to discuss it with his parents first.[2] The meeting between Joan's parents and the man who had shot her was understandably awkward, but remained civil enough. Burroughs, for his part, was angry with them for having never contributed to their daughter's wellbeing during most of her lifetime.

Burroughs got more bad news when he heard that his good friend, Phil White, had hanged himself in prison. White had turned stool pigeon on another prisoner in order to cut a deal, and when the authorities refused to hold up their end, he killed himself rather than face the consequences. He wrote to Ginsberg that his opinion of White still hadn't changed, despite sharing the same strong belief in the criminal code of ethics. He decided shortly after hearing the news that *Junky* would be dedicated to White.

2 Billy Jr. ultimately grew up with the Burroughses.

Soon after, good news came from Ginsberg, who, acting as literary agent, had gotten Burroughs' first book placed with A.A. Wyn, thanks to his friend from the nuthouse (yet another resident of Bellevue), Carl Solomon, who was working there as an editor. Both Ginsberg and Burroughs appeared to recognize the importance of writing as a way of exorcizing demons, although Burroughs was unhappy with the publishers' suggestion that he include Joan's death in his book, providing a weak argument against it to cover the fact that he simply was not ready to deal with the event, which is also notably absent from his letters. At the end of the book, he simply states, "My wife and I are separated."

Burroughs' correspondence during much of 1952 is dominated by discussions about his book, as well as *Queer*, which was partly written during that period and at times considered part of *Junky*, but wasn't published until thirty years later. Originally, Burroughs had included a great deal of "Reich and philosophical sections" which were "cluttering up the narrative," but these were removed, and with Ginsberg's help, they soon got the text ready for publication. It seems that at times, Burroughs was also eager to include some of his bizarre routines in *Junky*, although this was probably a protest at Wyn's demands to make the book more biographical.[3] To cover their backs, A. A. Wyn put out *Junky* with the memoirs of a narcotics agent, which at first offended Burroughs, but later he came to appreciate the choice and the book itself. He also appreciated the $1000 advance, and was in a good mood as Ginsberg had "relapsed," realizing the foolishness of his analysts. Burroughs wrote Kerouac, "I owe it all to Al Ginsberg. He is a real friend." Moreover, Burroughs was now a published writer, and with Kerouac's *The Town and the City*, and Ginsberg gaining recognition for his poetry, the three of them were heading for success. He was no longer alienated – he was at the center of a new literary movement.

Junky was ignored entirely by reviewers when published in 1953, but sold well. Sadly, for Burroughs, it made him only three cents per copy sold, and so it wasn't exactly a financial windfall. It can, of course, be seen as an important step in the

3 Some of them ended up in *Queer*.

career of a major American author. In *Junky* are the ideas and images that he continues to develop throughout the rest of his oeuvre. It is more autobiographical than his later works, as it began as an exercise in memory, and he was not yet confident enough in his abilities or his intuition to include much fiction. His book comes across as honest and objective, and details the laws of his society in the same way as Jack Black's *You Can't Win*. It was also stylistically inspired by detective fiction, which he had been reading for a number of years, with a particular fondness for Chandler and Hammett.

During this period, Burroughs had to sign in at the jail every week. Bail in Mexico meant probation, and although he was glad to have escaped any real punishment, it was time to move on. Marker soon left, as he was being watched by cops ever since the case. Burroughs again looked south, and considered a return to farming – perhaps in Ecuador or Panama. Again, as with his time in Texas, he is filled with ludicrous optimism. His failures at farming the first time around and his depressing stay in South America with Marker were evidently not enough to stop him assuming that everything would work out were he to buy a ranch and just throw everything into life in some random new country. One thing was for sure - he wasn't going to return to the "Repressive bureaucracy" of the U.S.

He was also considering a return to the pursuit of yagé and, despite it proving phenomenally unlikely, he maintained a hope that Marker would join him once again. One of his friends had told him that the American government was experimenting with it, and Burroughs immediately speculated: "Next thing will be armies of telepathy-controlled zombies marching around. No doubt about it. Yagé is a deal of tremendous implications, and I'm the man who can dig it." In another letter, he reiterated his determination: "*I must find the yagé.*" Leaving would mean losing the bond money posted to get out of jail, but he was itching to travel, and yagé had become his next obsession, and Burroughs' obsessions always took over his life, even if only for a short while.

In the meantime, Burroughs tolerated unpleasant visits from

Kerouac and Bill Garver, had his pocket picked of $200, and finally came to the realization that he would never get what he wanted from Marker. He was using black magic and curses as an attempt to win the favor of his lover, but he failed and gave up. Marker wouldn't return his letters or even say thanks for a birthday present that Burroughs sent. Then, his lawyer suddenly fled the country after killing a seventeen year old boy, and when his fellow lawyers attempted to fleece Burroughs out of more money, he realized that the time was right to do the same thing. As he'd fled America, it was now time to flee Mexico. It cost him his $2000 bond, but it was time for him to go south once again.

At the start of 1953, Burroughs was in Panama City, sick from withdrawal and a bad case of hemorrhoids. He spent four days in hospital to get them fixed, but still he bled every time he sat down, and was understandably in a foul mood during much of his time there. Later in the month he travelled to Bogotá, where he had the tremendous fortune of running into Richard Evans Schultes, a fellow Harvard graduate who just happened to be an expert on psychoactive South American plants. He was able to immediately show Burroughs a specimen, give him a brief lesson on the plant and its cultural significance, and said that he'd tried yagé, but hadn't had the full experience. Despite his amusement at Burroughs' pseudo-scientific approach, and his near religious devotion to the quest, he advised Burroughs to go deeper into the jungle and meet with the natives, if he really wanted to experience the intense and supposedly mystical trip that came with it. Schultes was able to help Burroughs by attaching him to a Cocoa Commission expedition that eventually put him in contact with a medicine man who was willing to give him the full yagé preparation.

What Burroughs wanted from yagé wasn't a high or a temporary escape. He wasn't looking to have fun, and it even went beyond his experiments that started with the chloral hydrate, into the effects of mind-bending substances. This time around, he was looking for something with a far greater promise. Yagé supposedly bestowed upon its user the gift of telepathy, and was tied into native mythology regarding the creation of the universe. Burroughs mostly hoped that it would prove able to "change fact." He had previously discussed with Ginsberg the validity of hallucinations and the effects of drugs, and to what extent these things qualified as "facts." Burroughs was likely seeking to change the past, at least in his own mind, by finding a drug with the ability to sufficiently alter his perceptions. This could be the only cure to his peculiar assortment of mental scars.

Indeed, yagé proved to him to be what they claimed about all drugs - it was utterly mind-bending and mind-expanding. He was motion sick from travelling through space and time, and he became different people. He could be and do anything, and he began to imagine the possibilities of it being used by people around the world. His sexuality changed, temporarily, and he was a full-blown heterosexual. He was possessed by a blue (or "blue purple") spirit. "The effect cannot be put into words," he wrote Ginsberg, in a letter that would eventually become part of a collection called *The Yagé Letters*. Of course, he attempted to put it into words shortly after:

> "It is not like weed or anything else in the world... It is the most powerful drug I have ever experienced. That is it produces the most complete derangement of the senses... The substance of the body seems to change... I feel myself change into a Negress complete with all the female facilities... Now I am a Negro man fucking a Negress... You are a man or a woman alternately or at will... I notice in lighter intoxication effect is Near East, the deeper intoxication the more South Pacific. There is suggestion here of phylogenetic memory of a migration from Middle East to South America to South Pacific... There is definite sense of space time travel that *seems* to shake the room."

Burroughs was clearly impressed by yagé, and suggested

bringing it back to the U.S. for further study, sensing it might have implications on the whole of society. Two days later, he continued to describe the drug's effects, in a style of writing more consistent with what people have come to expect from William S. Burroughs, literary figure.

> "Yagé is space time travel. The room seems to shake and vibrate with motion. The blood and substance of many races, Negro, Polynesian, Mountain Mongol, Desert Nomad. Polyglot Near East, Indian, and new races as yet unconceived and unborn, combinations not yet realized, passes through your body. You make migrations, incredible journeys through jungles and deserts and mountains (stasis and death in closed mountain valleys where plants grow out of your cock and vast Crustaceans hatch inside you and grow and break the shell of your body), across the Pacific in an outrigger canoe to Easter Island."

His writing in this July 10th letter to Allen Ginsberg is stunning. The visions are miraculous and the ideas wonderful and absurd. They are presented coherently, whilst at the same time reminiscent of his routines. He transitions from place to place effortlessly, indeed appearing to go through "space time travel" as he repeatedly said. As a writer, yagé had an instantaneous and powerful effect on his skills, and we can already see the mind that would soon create the masterpiece, *Naked Lunch*. His mood, too, appears to have lifted, and he seems at peace with the South American people, whom he previously described with some venom. "You are not the same after you have taken it," he says, and it appears that in his case he was right.

In the summer of 1953, Burroughs returned to the United States, first for a brief visit to his parents' house – where he was clearly unwelcome, despite still receiving his $200 a month – and then to New York, to visit Ginsberg. In the past few years, his correspondence with Ginsberg had been deeply important to Burroughs, who would otherwise have been isolated intellectually and emotionally. Particularly in regards the death of Joan, Ginsberg's support and lack of judgment had kept Burroughs going, and now he found himself in love with his young friend. Ginsberg clearly did not feel the same way, but out of respect he had sex with Burroughs. He found this deeply disturbing, however, as Burroughs would completely remove his "character armor" (a Reichian term) and become totally open. He became like a whimpering woman, Ginsberg thought. It was just as in his routines, where he completely took on another personality. Perhaps it was related to his experience with yagé, where he was able to become both genders. In addition to the weird sex that they had, Ginsberg was put off by the intensity of Burroughs' emotional attachment. During sex, Burroughs wanted to be completely possessed, but emotionally he wanted to possess the other person, absorbing them into himself – an act he called "schlupping." He opened himself entirely, as he had done with others before Ginsberg, leaving himself exposed and vulnerable, whilst at the same time desperate to consume the object of his affection entirely.

Ginsberg was glad when Burroughs left for Europe. He first visited his friend, Alan Ansen, in Rome, and then moved onto Tangier, which was to remain his home for the next three years. Burroughs knew that Paul Bowles, author of *The Sheltering Sky*, lived in Tangier, and he had also read Gore Vidal's *The Judgment of Paris*, which informed him of the city's permissive attitudes towards drug use and homosexuality. According to Ansen, after reading Vidal's novel Burroughs became determined to "steep himself in vice" in Tangier, echoing his excitement prior to visiting South America. Although not initially captivated by his new surroundings, Burroughs was able to easily acquire "boys and sweet opium" for cheap. When he turned forty shortly after arriving, he took stock of his life and was thrust into a crippling depression. He was still being supported by his parents, was still alone and without a sense of purpose, and was still haunted by various traumas. His life had been a series of disasters and mishaps, a long tragedy. He literally believed in demons and spirits and blamed these, and considered that a curse had been placed upon him. He told his biographer, Ted Morgan:

> "We assume that everything happens by accident. My attitude is that nothing happens by accident... The dogma of science is that the will cannot possibly affect external forces, and I think that's just ridiculous. It's as bad as the church. My viewpoint is the exact contrary of the scientific viewpoint. I believe that if you run into somebody in the street it's for a reason. Among primitive people they say if somebody was bitten by a snake he was murdered. I believe that."

Although this is Burroughs speaking some thirty years later, we can again see his desire to blame something else, some outside force, for all the suffering in his life. We also see his contradictory stance as he attempts to defend himself. The man who posited a philosophy called factualism, and claimed that everything not entirely proven by scientists as fact was without merit, is claiming that belief is enough, and criticizes science for only following the facts. Again, to Burroughs a fact is simply something *he* thinks, regardless of what anyone else says.

Magic, another fact for Burroughs, was a part of normal life in Tangier, and had been for millennia. The Moors believed in psychic power points and fertility cults, and the Muslims, when they came to power, held similar views, building their mosques on spots where they felt these powers were at their strongest. People viewed magic as just another element of reality, and used potions and curses regularly. They cast spells and went into trances. In the markets you could buy everything you needed to make a potion, and no one thought anything of it. Burroughs noted odd coincidences, too. He wrote to Ginsberg that, "This town seems to have several dimensions," and claims to have met several people each playing out different lives, like actors.

In Tangier Burroughs found people like himself – who'd made wrong turns at every point in their lives and ended up stranded in this odd city of the damned. But of course they were lowlifes, and soon enough he found himself entering their society. His letters detail a wild nightlife involving people who went there to escape and couldn't leave, who were all queers and junkies. More importantly, these people were *characters.* The criminals and addicts and losers were just made for a writer like Burroughs, and from the very start he was jotting down their over-the-top speech for magazine submissions that were never accepted. He was even taking note of absurd drunken rumors, like the "vicious, purple-assed baboons," that were supposedly keeping the writer Paul Bowles locked up in a castle. All of this will sound quite familiar to anyone who has read the author's later work, as Tangier quickly morphed into a fictional setting for his routines.

Here Burroughs became more obsessed with routines, which had cropped up throughout his life, especially when he was going through a time of some difficulty. They were obviously a way of getting his feelings out. Ginsberg speculated that it was because of repression in his childhood and that he developed these routines as a way of exploring his own mind and venting his troubles. Indeed, in an April 7th letter to Ginsberg, Burroughs connected routines to his own childhood, and claimed "without routines my life is a chronic nightmare." He also explains the process, claiming that routines couldn't work purely as a way of venting frustration or creating something by himself, but that he needed "a receiver" – a person who would listen to him while he went through the routine aloud. He says that if he doesn't have a receiver, the routine tears him apart inside, and in the letter, he scores out an apt description – "like homeless curse." Then he goes on to talk about an attempt to write a new novel, indicating that the two are linked. That novel, of course, was the genesis of *Naked Lunch.*

Still Burroughs had his usual sense of alienation, and his standard complaints. He went for a period without hearing from Ginsberg, and the sensation was not unlike junk withdrawal. He met with Paul Bowles but felt the man was cold, and he believed that Bowles was ignoring him, saying, "He invites the dreariest queens in Tangier to tea but never invited me." In the town's most popular bar, the barman seemed to take a dislike to Burroughs, and at the most popular restaurant, the 1001 Nights, he failed to connect with proprietor, Brion Gysin, who Burroughs thought wanted to "cut" him. Burroughs also disliked the locals, who he believed were sticking their noses into his business, and who he viewed as dirty and dishonest. Put simply, his attitudes were much the same as they were wherever he went.

In the summer of 1954, Burroughs wrote to Kerouac and mentioned studying Tibetan Buddhism, Zen, and Taoism. He talks about having studied yoga many years before, and recommends jiu-jitsu, although he claims that none of these are an answer to anything. Amusingly, in another letter he admits to have studied most of these things "in my usual sloppy way," and compares the adventures to his farcical journeys in South America. "Buddhism frequently amounts to a form of psychic junk," he says, which is particularly rich coming from a man who was so readily addicted to junk, psychic or otherwise. It holds no answers for people in a Western country, he says, and reiterates his faith in Reich and Spengler. His primary disagreement with Buddhism is that you must "remove love from your being in order to avoid suffering," but it is wrong to miss out on something as important as love for as shallow a goal as the avoidance of suffering.

He developed two new obsessions around this time: One was a boy named Kiki, who became Burroughs' sole companion. Burroughs seemed to have learned a little from his errors in the past, and although he came on too strongly, he held back more than with others and Kiki stuck around. Still, he left himself open and Kiki would say cruel things that brought him to tears. "I always have a fear with anyone I love that they really hate me and that I will suddenly be confronted with their hate," he said, adding, "Kiki always says afterwards he was only joking." The other obsession was Eukodol, a synthetic German form of morphine whose production had been discontinued, but which could be found in Tangier. Burroughs quickly developed a habit and found himself utterly hooked. It was the best junk he'd ever come across. As his dependence grew, he nearly burned down the town's supply, and the police were putting his acquaintances under surveillance. Burroughs' physical condition deteriorated, and when Kells Elvins came to visit, he thought Burroughs looked even worse than he had in Mexico City. When he tried to quit, he had to pay a friend to keep him locked up because he couldn't control himself, and eventually he became so sick that Kiki had to nurse him.

Burroughs was on and off junk, viewing it as a hindrance to his writing career. On junk he simply couldn't write, but off it he was too sick. He was writing Ginsberg as much as three times a day, too, unable to kick that particular habit. Soon he began to view Tangier as a possible location for his next book, and routines – which he sent to Ginsberg as his receiver – as a literary form. His letters from the period contain large portions of what eventually turned out to be *Naked Lunch*. Although he'd been writing them down over the years, he'd never really seen their potential, but now it was clear. The novel would be unpublishable, he knew, but he would write it nonetheless. He had found his voice. "This book is a must," he wrote as nuclear bombs were being tested above ground in the United States, "for anyone who would understand the sick soul, sick unto death, of the atomic age." The routines poured out of him, and he even mentioned to Ginsberg the possibility of bringing Joan's death into it when first exploring the O'Brien and Hauser section, but quickly dismissed the idea because of a fear of what he would discover. The words were coming from "a hostile, independent entity," perhaps the demon that took possession of him. He once described this style as "automatic writing," and later thanked Kerouac, whose "Essentials of Spontaneous Prose" had been tremendously influential upon him.[4] His writing was further

---

4 Interestingly, Jack Kerouac's own writing techniques were in part influenced by those of L. Ron Hubbard, who was well-known in the United States both for his science fiction and his growing pseudo-scientific therapeutic method, Scientology, but whose work was as yet unknown to William S. Burroughs. Hubbard claimed to have taped sheets of paper together and would speed-type entire books in a matter of days. He also called his process "automatic writing," although it is unlikely Burroughs ever came to realize this connection. Burroughs' own interest in Kerouac's method was, he claimed, "absolute, direct transmission of *fact* on all levels."

helped when he took a dolophine cure that gave him useful visions and a vital energy boost. In addition, he had a pleasant meeting with Bowles and Gysin, and Bowles seemed to have warmed to him a little.

Then, in early 1956 he took Dr. Dent's apomorphine cure in London, and managed to kick his habit again. He remained a proponent of this treatment, which used apomorphine as a metabolic regulator to treat addiction, for the rest of his life. He travelled Europe, returning to Tangier in September on a health kick, and developed an obsession with rowing. He even built himself another orgone accumulator, which looked much like a dog kennel. Without junk in his system, he began writing intensively. He wrote all day, smoking weed and laughing hysterically. He was transcribing routines that simply came to him, with no real aim or purpose. It was his "word hoard." Paul Bowles, with whom Burroughs was now friends, said that the floor of the apartment was covered in hundreds pages of writing when he visited. The pages were scattered everywhere, in no order, and often stepped on or covered in food. Jack Kerouac testified to this when he visited in early 1957, and volunteered to help Burroughs with typing and editing the book, although he found the material highly disturbing. When Kerouac asked him why it was so full of shocking images and ideas, he explained in a somewhat contradictory manner:

> "I get these messages from other planets. I'm apparently some kind of agent from another planet but I haven't got my orders clearly decoded yet. I'm shitting out my educated Middlewest background once and for all. It's a matter of catharsis, where I say the most horrible things I can think of."

To Jack, the book was taking over Burroughs. His conversation was overwhelmed by routines and he said the craziest and most disturbing things, so that Kerouac genuinely feared Burroughs had lost his sanity and would commit some awful atrocity.

The day before Kerouac left for America, Ginsberg arrived with his new lover, Peter Orlovsky. Soon Alan Ansen joined them, and they all set to work typing and editing Burroughs' book. They spent six hours a day for two whole months working on the book, with Ansen in particular demonstrating an ability to bring coherence to the otherwise disorganized stream of fantasies.

Burroughs was alone once again after his friends left in July, and went to Copenhagen to visit Kells Elvins. This visit was significant in that it provided him with the final location for his novel. So far he had incorporated the United States, South America, and Tangier (Interzone), but now there was a place called Freeland, based upon the soulless wasteland that Burroughs found Scandinavia to be. He stayed for nearly two months, with the words coming faster than he could write them down.

Upon returning to Tangier, Burroughs learned that Kiki had been murdered by a jealous lover, and that Bill Garver, another of his friends, had died in America. Burroughs felt that death was all around him. There was even a plane that crashed as it departed from the city, leaving no survivors. He kept writing, and was so involved in his work that he could hardly tell fact from fiction. The violence around him mirrored the violence in the book. He felt himself transforming, as the characters transform throughout *Naked Lunch*. Writing was like analysis, as he worked through his issues on paper. For one thing, he decided that he was no longer homosexual. He had cured himself through writing.

Burroughs escaped to Paris at the start of 1958, joining Ginsberg at the fabled Beat Hotel, where he took a room for $25 a month. Ginsberg had been worried about meeting Burroughs again. In Tangier Burroughs had been demented and at one stage Ginsberg had come at him with a carving knife to stop Burroughs from attacking Orlovsky. But when they sat down, Burroughs explained that he had changed, and that he wanted to "clear up psychoanalytic blocks." He claimed to have found peace within himself, was meditating, and had exorcised some of his demons through his fantasies, which involved brutally murdering Ginsberg and Orlovsky. He believed that by running through these fantasies, acknowledging them as real parts of himself, he had removed their ability to cause him or anyone else harm. Unbeknownst to either man, Burroughs had stumbled upon one of the central notions of a movement that was gaining popularity in the United States, L. Ron Hubbard's Dianetics. There was still at least one thing that for Burroughs was too awful to "clear," (to use Hubbard's terminology, of which Burroughs was not yet aware) and that was the incident with his nanny. It was still a source of darkness so grave that it gave him shivers, and was entirely blocked from his memory. Together, he and Ginsberg attempted to meditate and work through the issue, but Burroughs became so dark that he stopped, as Ginsberg feared for his life. Determined to fix himself, Burroughs began seeing a psychoanalyst, Dr. Marc Schlumberger, president of the Paris Psychoanalytic Society.

At the Beat Hotel, Burroughs was once again the wise man to the hip young kids. This time it spread further, as he became associated with the Beat Generation, a new phenomenon that was hitting newspapers around the world. When excerpts from *Naked Lunch* were published the *Black Mountain Review* and the *Chicago Review*, his underground reputation grew even greater, and finding the time to write proved harder. He dealt with unwanted visitors by staring at them and visualizing their departure. This usually made the person so uncomfortable that they left, again proving to Burroughs the power of telepathy and the human mind (and of course it had nothing to do just being rude or creepy). The excerpts published in the *Chicago Review* proved so incendiary that the publication collapsed under them, with the editors starting up a new publication, called *Big Table*, and running more excerpts because of all the publicity. Burroughs was becoming infamous. This infamy made the book all the more attractive to Maurice Girodias, the owner of Olympia Press, already noted for its controversial titles, such as Vladimir Nabokov's *Lolita*.

In Paris Burroughs befriended an eccentric cripple called Jacques Stern, who was fantastically wealthy and claimed to be a part of the Rothschild family. Stern liked to tell stories that it's hard to imagine anyone believing, but Burroughs – at least for a while – believed them all. The two men were actually rather similar, "both graduates of Harvard and junk," as Burroughs put it. Burroughs was able to tolerate Stern's monstrous tantrums and came to think of him as a genius: "The greatest writer of our time." He was also a Scientologist, and by some accounts encouraged Burroughs to undergo auditing. Burroughs' interest in Stern was typical of his gullibility and obsessive nature, and was somewhat of a practice run for his relationship with another important figure in his life.

In late 1958, Brion Gysin moved to Paris, ran into Burroughs, and took up the Beat Hotel. Ginsberg had left in the summer, and in his absence Burroughs found a new companion. He had never fully warmed to Burroughs in Tangier, but they quickly hit it off this time around, and Gysin was to prove immensely important in the development of Burroughs as a writer. He was a talented painter with an abnormally large ego, and liked to tell tall tales, making everything in his life sound dramatic. He even transformed his first meeting with Burroughs, which likely neither man would've remembered, into something surreal and paranormal, claiming Burroughs "trailed long vines of Bannisteria caapi [yagé]," and emitted a "blue light." Like Burroughs, he was terminally paranoid, interested in the fantastic and the bizarre, and had a view of reality that incorporated the magical. When things went wrong, the universe was to blame, or some wayward curse. Gysin's intense misogyny was even greater than Burroughs', and he soon had Burroughs back chasing men instead of women, convinced that women were inextricably tied to the systems of control that were gripping the world.

The suggestible and ever-gullible Burroughs fell immediately under Gysin's wing, as though the painter had cast a spell upon him. He was especially captivated by the story of Hassan ibn Sabbah, leader of a religious sect from the eleventh century in what is now Iran. Legend had it that Sabbah lived in a mountaintop castle, from where he telepathically commanded an army of assassins fed on hashish. He supposedly coined the phrase, "Nothing is true, everything is permitted," which Gysin loved and Burroughs immediately took for his personal motto. A little research would've led Burroughs to discover that the phrase was actually from a fictionalized account of Sabbah's life by French novelist, Betty Bouthoul, and that Gysin's version of Sabbah bore almost no resemblance to the genuine article – a man who enforced Shariah law so strictly that he had one of his own sons executed for drinking alcohol. But for Burroughs, a fact was something that sounded good, something he wanted to believe.

Gysin seems to have further altered Burroughs' views on the nature of reality, and he wrote to Ginsberg that Gysin's paintings defied reality and opened up holes in space (adding, apparently without humor, that it was for this reason that nobody would buy his work). Gysin also taught Burroughs that anything that was dreamed could become real, and Burroughs lamented the fact that more people were not "dreaming on the Gysin level." He said, for example, that if he dreamed of money or opium, he would wake up and it would simply appear for him. "There is nothing," he said, "that can stop the power of a real dream."

Together, they shared many supernatural experiences at the Beat Hotel. The first such incident occurred after Burroughs bought a keychain from a magic shop, and when they looked into the steel ball on the end, they both saw exactly the same thing – a Muslim funeral at Brion's old restaurant. Later Burroughs felt the ball had some sort of power that pushed him around his room, and began sleeping with the light on. Then they tried mirror gazing, which involved staring into a mirror for twenty-four hours. Burroughs saw a vision of his own hands, only weirdly distorted and pink, but was distracted when someone burst into his room. The visitor was shocked when he saw Burroughs' actual hands, which had come to resemble the odd mirror version. Another time, Gysin demonstrated for several visitors a trick which he claimed to have learned from a desert tribe, called face-vanishing. At first he wore a djellabah and his face entirely vanished, so you could see through his whole head, and then the image flickered for a while. Later, without the djellabah he was able to dissolve his features to an extent that he was effectively unrecognizable. Burroughs tried it, and was able to morph his face to become other people, including Paul Bowles. They also experimented with telepathy, and it seemed everyone was sharing visions. Burroughs, for his part, was seeing "Beautiful pink and black landscapes," and "flying saucers like flat fish full of black fuzz." Rumors were spreading about the odd goings on the Beat Hotel.

In July, when Girodias handed Burroughs a sudden ten day deadline to finish *Naked Lunch*, it was Gysin and the poet, Sinclair Beiles, who helped him to compile the final version. The publisher's office was a few blocks away, and sections were sent away when finished, and then onto the printer in random sequence, which worked just fine for Burroughs: "How random is random?" he asked. The book was intended to be read in any order. It had no beginning, middle, or end. It was always going on. Burroughs even designed the cover himself, having learned to draw from Gysin.

Naked Lunch threw Burroughs into the limelight. Even his parents now knew he was a writer, and they were not amused. He was barred from returning home, with the threat of losing his $200 a month allowance. The international press made reference to him, and he was interviewed for *Life* magazine. He had finally made it as an author, and yet his most notable breakthrough was just around the corner.

On October 1st, Gysin was using a Stanley knife when he accidentally cut through a stack of newspapers. When the pieces came together, he laughed at the silly results. He didn't think much more of it than an amusing coincidence, but when he showed Burroughs later that day, the author had a sudden flash of inspiration. "I showed the first texts to Burroughs hoping to hear him laugh out loud as I had. He took off his glasses to reread them even more intently, saying: 'You've got something here, Brion.'" As he had broken the conventions of narrative with his *Naked Lunch*, he could yet go further. He felt it was possible to cut through time and meaning, to see more and understand things that were invisible from the surface. A book needn't only defy chronological order, it could quite possibly break through the problems that were inherent in language – an idea to which he had held firmly since first reading Korzybski. The possibilities were endless, and Burroughs was about to spend many years exploring the world through this technique.

For Burroughs, the cut-ups were also tied into magic and control. Gysin, in an interview with Terry Wilson, explained:

> "They produced a certain kind of very unhappy psychic effect... They were the sort of texts you might use for brainwashing somebody, or you might use them for the control of an enormous number of people whom you drove mad in one particular way by one sort of this application of this dislocation of language, where by sort of breaking off all their synaptic attachments to language you would maybe acquire a social dominance over them..."

Soon Burroughs was putting in entire days of work dedicated to producing cut-ups. He cut-up his letters to the point that no one knew what he was trying to say, and mixed his own words in with those of other authors, and from sources like newspapers. Even the *Life* magazine article on the Beats was cut-up, becoming "Open Letter to Life Magazine." He was absolutely convinced of the significance of this discovery. Paul Bowles thought it was ludicrous, and that Burroughs was merely under the influence of Gysin, for whom this lunacy would not be such an unusual pursuit. Soon his other beliefs became tangled into the cut-ups. His idea that nothing is accidental came to influence his interpretation of the results of cut-ups, and he felt that the results could prophesize or influence future events. The cure for cancer, he thought, would be discovered by cutting together medical articles. Again, Burroughs was largely finding what he wanted to find, such as when a cut-up read, "What sort of eels called Retreat 23," he later read a newspaper headline that said, "A sixth army spokesman stated two more bodies recovered from the Eel River. Deaths now total 23," and was convinced that he'd seen the future.

The story of Burroughs' discovery of the Cut-up Method is now part of literary history. However, the image of Gysin cutting through the newspapers, then informing Burroughs, who was immediately struck by the brilliance of this technique and its myriad possibilities, is missing something. Burroughs did not simply have a flash of inspiration or intuition. Rather, the Cut-up Method stemmed from something else Gysin had taught him in the months prior to the incident with the Stanley Knife – something that took off from Burroughs' previous obsessions and his life experiences, mixing with Reich and Korzybski to inform his developing views on control and language. When Gysin related the story of his first cut-ups, Burroughs was thinking about L. Ron Hubbard and his Church of Scientology.

Preclear:

1959-1967

The importance of Scientology in Burroughs' life is somewhat undermined by the absence, in his biographies and collections of correspondence, of specific dates and details regarding just how he first came to learn about it. His biographies overlook the topic entirely until the late sixties, and his collected letters show a sudden interest, minus any real details, beginning around the fall of 1959. Instead, it is the Stanley Knife incident that has become legend, and the accidental discovery has gone down in literary history. It was a story retold by Burroughs and Gysin numerous times, and has worked its way into almost every book about the two men, thanks to the importance of the Cut-up Method in their work, as well as its influence upon other artists. It has come to overshadow Burroughs' discovery of Scientology, which in fact occurred before the Cut-up Method, was of more interest to him than this new literary technique, and in fact influenced its development. Add to this the fact that Gysin had only recently informed Burroughs of a number of outlandish ideas, like the Hassan ibn Sabbah tale, and it is hardly surprising to see Scientology sidelined.

Getting to truth is made more difficult due to a confusing description of events given by Gysin's biographer, John Geiger. His book, *Nothing is True; Everything is Permitted*, is a valuable resource due to its author having placed some importance on the story of Gysin's own brief interest in Scientology. Yet, his work has been mined for information by Burroughs scholars, who have all too often come to erroneous conclusions. One particularly well-known quote has added to the confusion. From an interview with Burroughs, in which he sought to gain details in order to pad out his description of a story relating to Gysin's first encounter with Scientology, Gieger wrote:

> "On his last visit to 1001 Nights, Burroughs was standing by the door, waiting for someone to pay the bill, when he spotted two rather strange looking people. 'There was something portentous about it, as though I was seeing them in another medium, like they were sitting there as holograms,' Burroughs remembered."

These portentous holograms were Mary and John Cooke, early Scientologists who were responsible for teaching Gysin about Scientology. Gieger's book is rather vague at this point and although Burroughs was tied in more for narrative effect than anything else, the absence of any specific details has led to the conclusion that Burroughs actually met and learned about Scientology from these people. It is likely that Burroughs just saw the Cookes and later, having heard about them through Gysin and learned about Scientology, saw some significance in his having noticed them. Indeed, it would have been hard not to notice them. By all account, these people were weird-looking. Early hippie-types, they wore bizarre clothes and covered themselves in jewels. It all fit very well into the mythology of Brion Gysin.

This information has been taken and used in an extremely popular online essay, which claims to explore Burroughs' interest in Scientology. Unfortunately, this essay further confuses the matter by placing Burroughs' encounter with these people in 1959, despite Gysin's restaurant having closed down more than a year earlier, with Burroughs and Gysin now at the Beat Hotel in Paris. Gieger's book also portrays that event as the Cookes' first visit, and they arrived in Tangier in late 1955 or early 1956. The author likely made the error because the first evidence of Burroughs' interest in Scientology appears in a letter to Allen Ginsberg, included the collection edited by Oliver Harris, on October 7th, 1959. The excitement which Burroughs shows indicts that he had only recently heard about Scientology, and obviously led the author of the essay to his mistaken conclusion. This essay relies heavily upon information from these letters and from Geiger's biography due to a lack of information in other texts and, in the absence of any specific references in more credible texts, it has been given more credence than it should have received. In particular, it has helped make famous online the quote that otherwise lay buried in Geiger's book.

To uncover the truth, which is in fact not particularly complicated, we need to go back to 1950:

John Cooke was, as Gysin described him, a "mystical" child, who, like Burroughs, had possessed a fascination with magic and the occult since an early age. Using his family's fortune, he travelled the world, seeking out spiritual figures and studying tarot cards – one of his lifelong obsessions. In 1950, he came to join a new movement called Dianetics, yet it was not due to his pursuit of the weird and fantastic. It was thanks to his first wife, Millen Cooke, who, while pregnant with his child, ran off to New York to join up with the Dianetics people.

Dianetics can be viewed as the predecessor to Scientology. In 1950, former science fiction and fantasy author, L. Ron Hubbard, contributed an article called "Dianetics" to the May issue of *Astounding Science Fiction*, and at nearly the same time his book, *Dianetics: The Modern Science of Mental Health* was published. These works, which were previously rejected by the medical establishment, set out the basic principles behind Hubbard's theories, which can be considered the central tenants of Scientology, to be elaborated upon and developed over the coming years. A month earlier he had established the Hubbard Dianetic Research Foundation, and immediately people were drawn to his ideas. His book was a best-seller, and people traveled far and wide to gain counseling – which became known as auditing or processing – from Hubbard and his fast-growing group.

Cooke followed his wife to New York, where he fell in with the Dianetics organization and met his second wife, Mary Oser, who had travelled from Switzerland to be audited. He impressed them by mastering their systems, and later claimed to have been the organization's first "clear" – which was then the ultimate goal of people in the Dianetics movement. Cooke became close to Hubbard and helped him to grow his movement, which was exploding in popularity – and controversy – during its early days. He later referred to it as a "billion buck scam," as he became increasingly aware that Hubbard's interest lay in making money from Dianetics. One criticism of Scientology today, which was not well-known in the fifties, is that followers are required to pay for their processing, and Hubbard is said to have withdrawn significant amounts of cash from his organization for his own personal use.

Soon, predictably, the movement ran into financial trouble, as well as investigations into the legitimacy of Hubbard's claims. Cooke was proud of his contribution to the movement, and claimed to have given Hubbard what he needed to succeed. In 1952, as Dianetics, the self-help pseudo-science, flailed and died, Cooke suggested that Hubbard should rebrand as a Church. In doing so, Dianetics became the Church of Scientology, and ceased having to pay taxes or justify its methods of therapy to the medical establishment.

When the Cookes appeared in Tangier in late 1955 or early 1956, reputedly on the advice of a Ouija board, John was still practicing Hubbard's methods, but he was not a member of the

Church. Indeed, it would have been hard for him to believe the rhetoric and propaganda that he had helped create. Nonetheless, he was what the Church considered a "squirrel" – that is one who practices Hubbard's methods and ideas without actually joining the religion.

Immediately, Gysin took a liking to John, although he despised "Scary Mary," as he called her. Clad in jewels, with John sporting a shaved head and a large beard, they supposedly burst into his restaurant crying "Guess where we came from and guess who we are!" before giving Gysin a giant emerald.[1] In other words, these were Gysin's kind of people. His first impression was that they were "really Magic People." John was, as Gysin later described, "a practicing magician on a private income... born rich and far out in a family of rich far-out people from the Hawaiian Islands, descended from millionaire missionaries." More importantly, they had no shortage of money, and at 1001 Nights, business was suffering. The Cookes ate and drank at the restaurant, spending a fortune and holding lavish parties there that kept the business afloat.

In the summer of 1956, Gysin temporarily closed 1001 Nights and followed the Cookes – at their request – to a villa on the Algerian coast. John had joined a Muslim sect but soon wanted out, feeling that their form of black magic was too much for him. When he tried to leave, they put a curse on him, using a white silk shawl. As soon as it touched his shoulders, he felt as though a scorpion had stung him, and soon he lost the use of his legs. He remained paralyzed for the rest of his life. The Cookes paid Gysin to come visit them and entertain John, and due to his financial situation, Gysin agreed. They even requested that Hubbard come to cure John, but instead, Hubbard sent his right-hand man, Jim Skelton, who reputedly lessened the damage but couldn't fully heal Cooke. Gysin carried Cooke about on his back, from doctor to doctor, and at Mary's request shaved his head and grew a beard in order to look like him. He listened to Cooke's lectures on Scientology, and put this to practice by auditing visitors to "Villa Cooke." Cooke said that Gysin was a "natural 'clear' and born 'operating thetan'" – two states that

1 It should be kept in mind that Gysin liked to exaggerate.

Scientologists aspire to achieve. He was reputedly promised that he would "go right to the head of the class and make all sorts of easy money."

Gysin returned to Tangier in December to reopen 1001 Nights, but things were about to take an unfortunate turn. Mary had callously ditched her crippled husband and taken up with Jim Skelton, then had bought out Gysin's partner in business, giving her complete control over the restaurant. In January, 1957, Mary told him, "You can go now," as he lost his restaurant. Gysin cried and remained broken by this incident for years. However, for him it wasn't just Mary's fault. Before losing it, he had found a packet hidden the restaurant's kitchen, containing all the requisite items for a curse that would drive him out for good. To Gysin, it didn't matter that the business had been dying from mismanagement even before the Cookes' intervention, or that one of his friends had broken in and robbed the place during his absence. It was a great conspiracy against him by dark forces.

After touring the world with his artwork during 1957, he moved to Paris in late 1958, running into Burroughs, and then moved into the Beat Hotel in 1959, where they explored the magical universe together, as detailed at the end of the previous chapter. Although Burroughs never explicitly stated when he was introduced to Scientology, he has said in interviews that Gysin taught him about it, and from the timing of his first letters that mention Scientology, we can assume that this occurred in the fall of 1959. It remains strange, then, that Gysin never shared with his new friend the secrets of Scientology until the fall of that year, or if he did, then Burroughs never thought it worthy of mentioning until October, and in particular until just days after discovering the Cut-up Method, which itself was absent from his correspondence – at least not explicitly mentioned - until December, a full two months later. Brion and his ideas are mentioned frequently and excitedly throughout the year leading up to October, with absolutely no mention of Scientology.

However, this presupposes the fact that Gysin was still infatuated with Scientology, and that it constituted part of what he wanted to teach Burroughs. On the contrary, Gysin "was never involved" with Scientology as a movement, but maintained a slight interest in Hubbard's ideas. As Gysin learned about Scientology from John Cooke, he was aware of certain elements of the church that detracted from the credibility it may have had for those who had learned about it elsewhere. Having met with L. Ron Hubbard and become disillusioned, Cooke had openly referred to it as a money-making scam. Of course, he still maintained that some of its ideas were worthwhile, otherwise he wouldn't have asked Hubbard to come and heal him, or continued for so long as a squirrel. Gysin, therefore, was no adherent of the religion, but thought it interesting and useful. It was probably not the first thing he thought to tell his new friend, who would listen and believe just about anything he said. Gysin ran through the things which were of greater interest to him first – magic, Hassan ibn Sabbah, the evils of women - coming only to Scientology later. It should be noted, then, that when Gysin passed along information about Hubbard's ideas, he was probably impressing upon his friend the value of Dianetics, or Scientology as a science of the mind, and not Scientology as a religion. He wouldn't have known that all the events in Burroughs' life had primed him for such a thing, making Scientology easily as appealing as Korzybski or Reich.

But that Burroughs was primed for discovering Scientology is beyond doubt. If one were to tailor a system of belief to his particular set of interests and problems, then surely the result would be something remarkably similar to Scientology. The casual reader will see from his work that Burroughs' mind was full of darkness. From childhood traumas to social dysfunctions, from homosexuality to drug abuse, from killing his wife to the countless friends he'd lost to violent deaths, Burroughs' life was one of pain. He had a head full of traumatic memories, and his beliefs and obsessions indicate a constant search for a cure. He was thus vulnerable, but still intelligent enough that he would not simply accept any old system. For all Burroughs fell for a number of scams, he resisted others. He was a sucker for anything scientific-sounding, though, and in Hubbard's words he found a similarity to his own; an echo of factualism and the self-justification of a man overly determined to prove himself correct. Scientology offered everything Burroughs needed, and it claimed to do so with ease.

On October 7th came the first recorded instance of Burroughs mentioning Scientology. He writes to Allen Ginsberg:

> "Remembering has many levels. We remember our operations under anesthesia according to *L. Ron Hubbard – DIANETICS –* went on to *Scientology*, which you would do well to look into. A run in time, you know. Remember I gave you a tip, said the Waiter."

Near the end of the letter he reminds Ginsberg: "don't forget to give Hubbard a run for his money," and after his name, adds to the letter "Hello – Yes – Hello."

Although Burroughs does not explicitly mention having read Hubbard's book, and he could well have learned enough from Gysin to have written this letter, his later comments imply that by this point he already had. Regardless, it is important that his first mention of this new idea concerns memories, an extremely significant part of Hubbard's book, and central to both Dianetics and Scientology. In *Dianetics*, he explores the complexity of the human capacity for remembering, and outlines a theory of disease based upon memories. His ideas sound quite similar to Reich's notion of psychosomatic illness caused by societal repression. Traumatized for life by something dark in his childhood, as well as more accessible memories, Hubbard's theories would certainly have held some degree of promise. As with his search for yagé, Burroughs was always seeking to "change fact" by removing or altering unpleasant memories.

Hubbard's book centers around the notion of the "reactive mind" – "a portion of a person's mind which works on a totally stimulus-response basis." In this part of the brain, "engrams" are stored. He described engrams as:

> "A mental image picture of an experience containing pain, unconsciousness, and a real or fancied threat to survival. It is a recording in the reactive mind of something which actually happened to the individual in the past... It must, by definition, have impact or injury as part of its content. These engrams are a complete recording, down to the last accurate detail, of every perception present in a moment of partial or full unconsciousness."

The reactive mind is simple and lacks the critical abilities of the conscious mind. Therefore, engrams hold much more power over people than they should, and one cannot control an engram's reaction to a stimulus. They don't adhere to logic or reason, and cause people to be destructive, fearful, or to develop illnesses. The aim of Scientology is to "run" engrams and thereby remove them from the reactive mind. This is achieved through auditing, and can involve the use of an E-meter. The E-meter is a device designed to measure resistance between the analytic and reactive minds, and therefore to isolate the trauma. Through repeated isolation, the engram can be expunged. A person whose engrams have been run is what Scientologists call a "clear." Hubbard makes extraordinary claims about the abilities of clears throughout his book, such as that a clear cannot suffer from a cold, because colds are psychosomatic illnesses. Like Burroughs, he believed this because of his own experiments, and considered it a fact.

Burroughs is being somewhat playful in his letter, teasing his friend. He is tossing out a new idea, vaguely referencing something that has interested him – that is Hubbard's theories on engrams and the reactive mind – and even makes two silly puns. Scientology texts use "run" as a description of the process which aims to clear engrams, and Burroughs, for whom the idea is clearly new and interesting, is playing with Ginsberg with this slight joke that his friend could not possibly get. The sign-off is a phrase that is used in Scientology auditing, and although it is reasonably well known today outside of the Scientology community – largely because of Burroughs and Gysin – it would also have remained cryptic to Ginsberg.

On October 27th, Burroughs wrote to Ginsberg again, and this time his tone has moved from playful to cold and exclusionary, and suggests a personal change within himself, as well as a gap in their friendship perhaps stemming from this change, when he says: "I sometimes feel that you have me mixed up with someone else doesn't live here any more." Burroughs' snide and childish tone is in part due to a disagreement between them in regards Burroughs' "Deposition" for *Naked Lunch*, in which Ginsberg felt he tried to "justify" the novel in unnecessarily serious terms, effectively detracting from its literary and cultural significance. However, with Ginsberg replaced as his receiver and emotional support by Gysin and Ian Sommerville, and with his literary reputation more or less secured by way of infamy, Burroughs is being callous.[2] He feels he no longer needs Ginsberg.

The idea that Ginsberg no longer understands his friend shows that Burroughs has come to identify with Scientology and the Cut-up Method so much that he has moved on and effectively become a new person.[3] His consciousness has changed, and he has progressed to a new state of being that his friend cannot comprehend. Burroughs suggests that Ginsberg carefully read a biographical note, which is clearly an early example of a cut-up. Given that Burroughs had by this point made no attempt to describe to Ginsberg what cut-ups were, one can only wonder at his reaction to the gibberish that is attached to the end of the letter. For Burroughs, though, it cut through reality to give a more accurate portrait of himself. Around this time he also wrote to his parents, telling them not to worry if his letters sounded strange, because language was evolving. "The old grammar forms no longer useful," he informed them. October 1959 was evidently the turning point in his war on language.

2 Ian Sommerville was Burroughs long-time lover. They met in Paris and stayed close until Sommerville's death in 1976.

3 Of course, this has been a complaint of many Scientology critics, and critics of other cults. The techniques employed by cult leaders, which were successfully used by Hubbard, often render adherents unrecognizable to their friends and family, and aim to instill in the adherents a distrust of their former acquaintances.

He goes on to talk about Scientology again, showing a better understanding of its primary ideas:

> "The method of directed recall is the method of Scientology. You will recall I wrote urging you to contact local chapter and find an auditor. They do the job without hypnosis or drugs, simply run the tape back and forth until the trauma is wiped off. It works. I have used the method, partially responsible for recent change in management, and policy…"

After signing off, he adds:

> "P.S. L. Ron Hubbard – Dianetics, Hermitage House, N.Y. 1950.
> "Movement now called 'Scientology'; used more for manipulation than therapy. Known to Russians since long time. Everybody – I mean on top level – now picking up. Southern California camouflage seemingly necessary. Last call to dinner."

Again, Burroughs' interest lies in memory, and specifically in removing trauma from the mind. This is something that would remain the focus of his interest in Scientology during the next decade, and would remain a part of his outlook even after his fascination with Scientology had drawn to a close. For him, Hubbard's reactive mind was like a recording device – you could go backwards and repeat something, or you could completely erase it. He briefly describes the ideas behind the E-meter, which was to become another of his obsessions, and says that he has been run – in other words, he'd taken steps towards erasing parts of his own memory that were causing him pain. We know that Gysin was experienced in auditing, and so it was possible that he conducted these sessions. When he says that he has effectively been cured, and that Scientology has changed his outlook on the world, he is again demonstrating an ability to jump headfirst into something. It is wishful thinking, as by this stage he would probably have undergone less than a month of auditing.

The second of the two above quotes suggests an early awareness of the dangers of Scientology. Burroughs has obviously found techniques that could help him, and clearly some of Hubbard's ideas match up well with Burroughs' own, but already he had recognized its capacity for social control. This appears to be about the extent of his critical thinking, and indeed was probably an idea related to him by Gysin, as in all other respects he was falling under this new spell. However, it is important to note that he was aware of the difference between Dianetics and Scientology – which is to say the pseudo-science and the religion that is based upon it. From the very start, Burroughs was fascinated by Hubbard's theories rather than his rules and systems of belief. He viewed Dianetics as an important discovery in the realm of mental health, whereas Scientology is a way of manipulating large numbers of people. This compares to his absolute certainty of the validity of Reich's scientific ideas, and his rejections of his social theories.

He solidifies his position by adding, "Schlumberger, needless to say, fell overboard like the cook and was left several centuries behind." This is a play on an old sailor's song lyric, and refers to his psychoanalyst, Dr. Marc Schlumberger, with whom Burroughs had been making great progress until his sudden conversion to the methods of Scientology. It is a clear dig at the whole psychoanalysis field, which Burroughs had come to view as badly outdated. Whilst this was something he had suggested years before, it no doubt helped him form a positive opinion of Hubbard's book, which begins with a stream of insults against modern techniques for dealing with what he describes as "aberrations," labeling these approaches "brutal" and "violent," saying, "they reduce the victim to mere zombiism, destroying most of his personality and ambition, and leaving him nothing more than a manageable animal." Again, this echoes Burroughs' earlier digs at the profession, and would strike as reasonable a man who had himself been locked up in Bellevue, along with his late wife and several of his friends.

Two days later Burroughs wrote to Ginsberg again, this time hinting at the Cut-Up Method, and tying it quite explicitly to Scientology:

> "I have a new method of writing and do not want to publish anything that has not been inspected and processed. I cannot explain this method to you until you have the necessary training. So once again and most urgently (believe me there is not much time), I tell you: 'Find a Scientology Auditor and have yourself run.'"

That Burroughs viewed Scientology as a prerequisite for understanding his cut-ups is fascinating, but yet unsurprising when we dig a little deeper. For him, these two discoveries were tied together. He came upon them around the same time, suggested by the same man, and they took off from his previous theories. At the heart of it, there was the word – a problem for Burroughs ever since reading Korzybski. The early pages of Hubbard's *Dianetics* are littered with Korzybski's ideas. Indeed, they appear before even Hubbard's ideas – in the "Important Note" at the beginning of the book, Hubbard demands the reader must understand each and every word in the book, in its context, before going further, or else he will not gain anything from reading. Although Hubbard has been accused of plagiarism and more subtle forms of idea-theft, he references Korzybski briefly in conjunction with the reactive mind (although Hubbard claims credit) and did later admit: "General Semantics was of use to *Dianetics*. I started going back looking for the first time a word had appeared... There might be some misdefinitions... General Semantics is definitely of use in the definition of a word."

For Burroughs, who never turned his back on General Semantics, these obvious references would have convinced him that Hubbard was onto something. They were both heading in the same direction. Hubbard's notion was that "words sometimes have several meanings" and that misunderstanding these words, or applying an inaccurate meaning, leads to an overall inability to comprehend the idea.[4] To this end, Hubbard included definitions of what exactly *he* meant by a particular word, in footnotes at the bottom of each page. He also indicates where commonly used words are insufficient, and changes them to more appropriate terms, such as "regression" becoming "returning." Later, in discussing the different kinds of memories, Hubbard suggests as optimal the ability to think in terms of sensation – that is to say, not in terms of words. This had been a technique which Burroughs attempted to adopt back in Chicago, in 1939, when he heard Korzybski lecturing. Hubbard also determined that the word functioned as a form of control, as a stimulus that could trigger engrams, causing the reactive mind to make predictable responses. For Burroughs, the Cut-up Method could well be viewed as a form of auditing as it disassembled language to remove from it the ability to elicit predictable responses, and thereby freed people from control. It must have appeared he had found a brother in the war against the tyranny of language. Burroughs was cutting through language to reveal true meanings, while Hubbard was changing language to reflect its true meaning.

At the end of this letter, Burroughs leaves off his usual "love" and simply signs his name. His last remark is "Pay no attention to above [referring to the comment about finding a Scientology auditor]. I know you won't anyway, and it isn't written for 'you' exactly." This snide remark suggests a frustration that Ginsberg hasn't immediately converted to his new views on life, again highlighting just how much faith Burroughs had already placed in Scientology.

The next day Burroughs wrote a somewhat more pleasant letter to Ginsberg, having received from his friend a packet of mescaline for which he had long been asking. Ginsberg had been skeptical about "these people," as he referred to the religion's adherents, but Burroughs made another attempt to justify his interest and to intrigue his old friend:

"I have had very practical contact with 'these

---

4 This idea was so important to Hubbard that not only does this quote appear in *Dianetics*, but also in many of his other publications.

people' they are very practical people... Jack
Stern was one of them...[5] The book [*Dianetics*]
itself is not interesting all important techniques
classified... But name dropping is very unchic
and very poor hygiene.
"Of course scientology attracts all the creeps of
the cosmos... You see *it works*."

Burroughs' interest in the "classified" techniques is hardly
surprising. Gysin must have enlightened him to the fact that
Scientology works on a system of hierarchy, with secrets
doled out based upon a member's progression in the religion
– and their financial investment. This would have appealed to
the old St. Louis side of Burroughs, which yearned for social
advancement, as well as to the young boy who was conned out
of his money to learn the secrets of mind control, as detailed in
"Personal Magnetism," the scarred and sick man seeking a cure
for his childhood and adult traumas, and to the amateur man
of science who'd blundered his way into botanical history in
South America. Overall, though, he seems impressed by these
"practical people" and toys with Ginsberg by refusing to name
names (other than Stern), whilst hinting without subtlety that
some very hip people are part of the movement.
　　Thus, by the end of October 1959 we have had four letters
in relatively short succession mention his newfound interest
in Scientology, demonstrating not just its importance to him,
but the speed with which he takes to it. He goes from a brief
and teasing mention at the start of the month, to statements
regarding its absolute effectiveness, and even claiming that it has
changed him as a person. Burroughs has alluded to an interest in
Scientology because of Hubbard's theories regarding memories
(and in particular dark and troubling memories), their purported
ability to remove trauma from the human mind, the supposed
superiority of this new approach to mental health over that of
psychoanalysis, and a shared interest in the use of language by
mysterious forces of control, as well as methods to combat this
control, which Burroughs perceived to be similar to his own.

5 Burroughs always used the Anglo version of Jacques' name in his letters.

We can add to this Hubbard's statements on the importance of facts: "a fact is never important without proper evaluation of it and its precise relationship to other facts." Hubbard's rhetoric regarding facts sounds surprisingly similar to Burroughs' own wild claims. Both men appear to take their ideas from the past, satisfy their own doubts, and then present their ideas as facts in light of overwhelming evidence (mere conspiracies, of course) to the contrary. Of course, Hubbard is very careful to put his "science of mental health" across as a bone fide science that is beyond reproach, and Burroughs, who fell for a Mexican truth serum and just about everything else that cropped up along his path through life, went for it hook, line, and sinker.

Additionally, Hubbard claims the ability to cure homosexuality, promises an improvement in intellect and imaginative power, explains away "evil" as a response to "wrong data," and even manages to incorporate and explain the presence of demons (it turns out they're not real, and simply parts of the mind perverted by engrams). To a man desperate for a cure to a great many troubles, always at war with himself, and now seeking a tool in the battle against the word, Scientology could not have been any more appealing.

In mid-November, Burroughs wrote Ginsberg again. Although he refrained from making direct reference to Scientology, he boasted of a "new method of writing." One could well assume he is talking about the Cut-up Method, which heretofore had been absent from his communications, but in the next line he says that in the future he will only publish "material subjected to the processing of new method." Given his familiarity with the basics of Scientology, it's hard to imagine that the use of "processing" was accidental.

Years later, Ginsberg would attempt to explain Burroughs' early fascination with the Cut-up Method, and he tied it firmly to the issues that drew Burroughs into Scientology:

> "In fact, the cut-ups were originally designed to rehearse and repeat his obsession with sexual images over and over again... so that finally

> the obsessive attachment, compulsion and pre-
> occupation empty out and drain from the image.
> In other words, rehearsing and repeating it over
> and over, and looking at it over and over, often
> enough. Finally, the hypnotic attachment, the
> image, becomes demystified."

What he is describing is, in fact, the auditing process, which required repetition as a means of removing traumas and troubles from the mind. Whether Ginsberg was aware of this similarity is unclear, but the process is unmistakable, and demonstrates a clear link between Scientology and the Cut-up Method.

At the Beat Hotel, Burroughs worked with Sinclair Beiles, Gregory Corso, and of course Brion Gysin on a book of cut-ups. Corso was ambivalent about the technique, and outright despised Gysin, but enjoyed working with Burroughs. They each contributed cut-ups which displayed their own voices, in what became *Minutes to Go*. Gysin came up with the name after being told that there wasn't much time left to finish the project, and also contributed a page of cut-ups of the one phrase: "Rub the Word Right Out." It displayed his desire to destroy language through cut-ups, which further upset Corso, but in Burroughs' eyes it was further proof of Gysin's genius. Beiles found private backers to fund the publication, and it was released in a limited edition run of a thousand copies in March, 1960, with ten copies printed for a special edition that was designed specifically for the reader to cut up.

In Burroughs' contribution, we can see his interest in Scientology mixing with his earlier fascination with language, to create what was becoming an important new dimension in his life and work: the word as a virus:

> "In THEE beginning was THE word... The word
> was a virus... 'Function always comes before
> form' L. Ron Hubbard. Virus made man... Man
> is virus... Kick that virus habit MAN."

Elsewhere he references the reactive mind ("any Haitian zombie with a Reactive mind") and Hubbard's notion that silence is necessary ("Ron Elroy Hubbard: Only absolute silence, utter silence and tomb-like silence, should attend an operation or injury of any kind").[6] The latter quote is actually taken verbatim from Hubbard's *Dianetics*.

In October of the previous year, Burroughs had admitted in court that he had been involved in a plan to smuggle cannabis, although the plan had never come to pass. His attorney managed to convince the judges that Burroughs was a true man of letters, and this fact was helped greatly by the recent publication of his "Deposition," which was to precede *Naked Lunch*, in *Nouvelle Revue Française*, a highly respected publication. He was portrayed as a decent literary fellow who had fallen in with bad company, and got off with an eighty dollar fine. Burroughs was glad to have been busted in France, rather than the United States, where laws treated drug users worse than murderers, and he was actually put in good stead by claiming to be an artist, rather than have the fact used against him. But a few months later he was hearing voices telling him to get back to the States, and then came a phone call from the U.S. Embassy. Burroughs was called in and told that he should get back to America before the French deported him. They said, "Keep your room clean," which put him on edge. His lawyer checked into the matter and said that there was no move to deport him, and soon Burroughs was convinced that there was a plan to raid the Beat Hotel, and that if nothing was found, evidence would be planted.

In April 1960, he moved to Earl's Court, in London, proclaiming once again that his new home was superior to others because people were capable of minding their own business. He continued to move forward with his cut-ups, staying in his room and working most of the time, or else relaxing in a

---

6 Silence is considered important in Scientology, due to Hubbard's theory that engrams are created by speech that is registered during times of unconsciousness. Another Korzybski-inspired idea, Burroughs was interested in the idea of silence as halting the word virus, and Hubbard's advocacy of muting internal speech (which he considered involuntary).

nearby cemetery. He had another book of cut-ups ready to send out, this time featuring only Burroughs and Gysin, called *The Exterminator*. He sent it to Dave L. Haselwood, a publisher in San Francisco, calling it "abstract literature observation and mapping of psychic areas," and explaining that it was "only a transcription of voice along the streets and quarters where I pass." Gysin, again, played with permutations of single phrases in an attempt to undermine the validity of the words, whereas Burroughs cut various forms of writing together, including news reports and magazine articles. Unsurprisingly, the books didn't sell. Haselwood put out an edition of a thousand copies, but no one was interested, and Burroughs blamed Haselwood.

It wasn't just his Cut-up Method that people were having difficulties with. Some of Burroughs' friends were opposed to his interest in Scientology. Chiefly, Sommerville was displeased and thought that Burroughs' intellect was wasted on such nonsense. Gysin later explained: "Ian says Bill is only interested in Scientology because he wants to have power over people." Whilst this is unlikely, it may well have contributed in some small way to his fascination. Again, this harkens back to the essay, "Personal Magnetism," in which the young Burroughs falls for a scam that promises the ability to "control others at a glance."

Several months later, having further developed his approach to the Cut-up Method, Burroughs assessed his technique with the first two books:

> "Often from a page of cut ups I will use one or two sentences. It depends on the material and purpose cut in. In *Minutes to Go* and *The Exterminator* I was using cut up material intact. At the time I had not learned to select. Also was more concerned with using the cut ups as fact assessing instrument."

In London, Burroughs set about working on his next book, *The Soft Machine*, which was largely composed from material left over from *Naked Lunch*. He referred to the giant body of text that had come about from his bursts of "automatic writing"[7] in Tangier as his "word hoard" – from which *The Ticket That Exploded* and *Nova Express* also came, although new material was added and cut in. At its core, *The Soft Machine*, one of his best known novels, is utterly inspired by Scientology. Hubbard's view of the reactive mind was appealing to Burroughs, who liked the idea of the human memory base as something that could be, in essence, wiped clean. His interpretation of Hubbard's theory was that the human body was one big recording device (literally, a soft machine) and that language was a tape that was being constantly fed through it by systems of control, imprinted with data that would elicit certain responses. The reactive mind, which Hubbard said (in another hand-me-down from Korzybski) "thinks only in identities," reacts predictably to these stimuli and thus humans are utterly at the mercy of the controllers.

Scientology is linked to another of Burroughs' obsessions, the Mayans, who also appear throughout his novels. In Burroughs' opinion, which contradicted the prevailing views of experts, the Mayan civilization was a place of violence, with a tiny percentage of the population under the absolute control of a handful of priests. These men used mind control by way of a calendar that would dictate how and what people felt:

> "I have explained that the Mayan control system depends on the calendar and the codices which contain symbols representing all states of thought and feeling possible to human animals living under such limited circumstances — These are the instruments with which they rotate and control units of thought — I found out also that the priests themselves do not understand exactly how the system works and that I undoubtedly knew more about it than they did as a result of my intensive training and studies — The technicians

---

7 In his *Astounding Science Fiction* article, Hubbard called his process "automatic writing," and said that its function was to draw otherwise unavailable information from the memory banks.

who had devised the control system had died out and the present line of priests were in the position of some one who knows what buttons to push in order to set a machine in motion, but would have no idea how to fix that machine if it broke down, or to construct another if the machine were destroyed — If I could gain access to the codices and mix the sound and image track the priests would go on pressing the old buttons with unexpected results."

In a chapter called "The Mayan Caper," Mayan priests play the role of the guardians of the control machine (in this case, the Mayan calendar), and Burroughs uses the Cut-up Method to destroy them. He photographs their books and records the sounds of agricultural operations, mixing it all strategically to cause their downfall. "Inexorably as the machine had controlled thought feeling and sensory impressions of the workers, the machine now gave the order to dismantle itself and kill the priests... You see the priests *were* nothing but word and image, an old film rolling on and on with dead actors." This all takes off from the notion of the reactive mind and human actions as utterly predictable, based upon the right set of stimuli. His war on the Mayan priests is used to indict success in the same sort of battle waged by L. Ron Hubbard – to break up the input of negative data that ultimately conditions humans to commit destructive acts, thereby becoming free.

Burroughs urged all-out war against the forces of control, and his weapon of choice, naturally, was the cut-up. It was a way of exposing the hidden meanings within existing language, and of robbing language of these meanings. Soon he was convinced that it wasn't just a literary technique: "Use of cut ups of course increases ability to cut with the eyes." Burroughs was asked by publisher and editor of *The Outsider*, Jon Edgar Webb, to contribute to the first issue of his now cult literary journal, and Burroughs sent him an early excerpt from *The Soft Machine*. Before and after its publication, he sent out excerpts in order to build publicity for himself and his work. Still early in his cut-up period, Burroughs did a lot of cutting, but relatively little selecting, and when the novel was published the following year, Burroughs was unhappy. He revised it twice more – with almost half of the book disappearing by the second edition, and a complete shift in the order of the story, one could argue that they constitute entirely different novels. For the third edition, published in 1968, he added "Appendix to The Soft Machine," in which he listed the tools necessary to fight the systems of control: Scientology, apomorphine, and Reich's orgone theories. These ideas are evident in the novel itself, through each of its incarnations.

In a letter to Gysin during the spring that includes a considerable amount of cut-up text, Burroughs plays with phrases and demonstrates the application of the Cut-up Method as a means of therapy, even tackling the previously difficult subject of Joan's death. He writes: "Ugly Spirit Shot Joan Because." Decades later, in the introduction to Queer, he claimed that it was Gysin who came up with the phrase in Paris, and speculated that it meant the possessing spirit had caused him to shoot Joan simply to make its presence clear. Later in the letter he mentions that "Scientologists have moved in next door."

In the summer of 1960, Burroughs' infatuation with Scientology had not yet abated, although he had for six months ceased hounding Ginsberg about it. He had taken to adding "Present Time" to the dates on his correspondence, something that comes again from Hubbard's *Dianetics*, and means being "in communication with [the] environment as it exists, not as it existed."[8] He also used "Past Time" where he felt it was appropriate. A great number of Burroughs' letters have this trait, and it's not difficult to see that it matches up well with the personality of the man who wrote *Naked Lunch* – a novel with no beginning, middle, or end, and was instead written so that it was always happening. These phrases obviously resonated with Burroughs, and appear throughout many of his books.

In July he wrote Dr. Dent to request permission to quote from

8 He had also taken to writing "Pre-sent Time" and "Just Time" as a means of playing with Hubbard's idea.

73

his book, *Anxiety and its Treatment*, as Burroughs was planning an article on the apomorphine cure. He took the opportunity to ask if Dent was aware of Scientology or Dianetics.

> "I wonder if you have any contact with the group here that is engaged in encephalographic research? Has any one gone into the pharmacology of brain areas, that is, made observations on what brain areas are stimulated by various pharmacological agents? Apomorphine? Mescaline? It would seem to be a most fruitful line of inquiry."

This is a very early example of Burroughs' own twist on Hubbard's engram theory. Reading Hubbard's book had changed and informed Burroughs' opinion on the brain, and he was now convinced of the reality of the reactive mind, and of engrams. Years later, he would suggest studies based upon exploration of the brain to pinpoint areas where engrams form, using "encephalographic equipment." For him, each obsession helped justify his others and form part of his overall world view. For example, the reactive mind proved to him that the Mayan priests could have exerted mind control powers via linguistics, and the apomorphine cure helped prove that the reactive mind had a physical location in the brain.

In a letter to Bill Belli, whom he met at the Beat Hotel in 1959, Burroughs wrote about humans as "out of date" and ends with the idea that human beings need to change – suggesting that this involves a radical rethink vis-à-vis language – in order to *"survive."* Hubbard's first point in Dianetics, upon which the rest of the book expounds, is that "Man is motivated *only* by survival." He also quotes Gysin in saying, "Rub Out The Word" and then references Mao Tse Tung's guerrilla war tactics. Clearly he is continuing and developing his ideas for an assault on language, not only for the sake of breaking free from control on a personal level, but for some global purpose.

In September he wrote Ginsberg again, elaborating on the Cut-up Method almost a year after its discovery. It is, ironically, one of the easier of his letters to understand, given that he didn't actually cut it up. He explains that he is becoming more selective with the process, using mostly poems by Rimbaud and St. Perse, and suggesting that one need only pick and choose specific lines from an entire page of cut-ups in order to fulfill a purpose: "no necessity to retain any material not pertinent." At the end of the letter, he once again mentions Scientology, asking Ginsberg after a nine month break, "Have you contacted Scientology-Dianetics? Ron Hubbard father of has headquarters here."

In the fall of 1960 Burroughs was now interested in the concept of "flicker." Originally Brion Gysin had come up with the notion of a "Dreammachine" after lying on his back on a bus in France, and the flicking of sunlight between overhanging branches had produced visions. He told this to Ian Sommerville who, in February, put together a crude machine with a lightbulb and a rotating piece of cardboard. It was later rebuilt and patented by Gysin. This was to be another in a long line of obsessions for Burroughs and crops up throughout his 1960s writings.

Around the same time, Burroughs also posited the idea of using a tape recorder to produce audio cut-ups, something that he would continue to do in future decades. He was always interested in new technology and using it as a means of beating the old systems of control. Sommerville, who was – at least compared to Burroughs – an expert in computers and other related technologies, helped a great deal in these early experiments. Burroughs used tape recorders so frequently and so vigorously that he was constantly breaking them, with some lasting only a few weeks. Soon he was working on improving the auditing process.

> "I have worked out a method of running on the tape recorder with cut ups. Will approach the scientologists in London. Get this show on the road. I cleara everybody."

A few months later he went into more detail in a letter to Ginsberg:

> "[Tape recorder cut-ups] can also be used as therapy. Write talk account of your illness. Now cut the page up. Now put it on tape recorder. Now cut back back over it. Get it outside your head. Wipe it off the tape. This is streamlining *dianetics* therapy system of running back and forth traumatic material until it is wiped off the tape and refiled as neutral memory. The use of tape recorder to facilitate this process and the use of cut ups is my idea. *It works. Try it.*"

He had associated Scientology and the Cut-up Method from for more than a year, but by now he clearly had studied Scientology enough that he believed he had actually developed upon Hubbard's ideas, and was planning to approach the London headquarters. He was thinking about improving the auditing process, demonstrating once again how interwoven these two concepts were in his head.

In November, Burroughs visited a Scientology center near his home and tried his hand at auditing. He managed to smuggle out some materials, including several "Preclear Assessment Sheets," indicating that he considered these of possible literary potential. On these sheets he filled out the date and his name, but the questions went unanswered. They were fairly standard for Scientology procedure, and centered on family, life, criminal activities, and even whether or not the preclear is using drugs or alcohol.

That same month he wrote Ginsberg yet again to attack psychoanalysis, displaying an interest in the effects of drugs, flicker, and Scientology auditing on the human mind:

> "When I think of the time and money wasted on the preposterous fraud of analysis and what they are paid to do nothing and determined to go on doing nothing. Have they picked up on the encephalographic research of Grey Walter?[9] He

9 Grey Walter was a neurophysiologist who had been performing experiment similar to Burroughs' in the area of flicker.

can remove so called hallucinations by direct brain area intervention. Have they picked up on scientology? On the new hallucinogens? Of course not. All they want is to sit on their fifty dollar ass."

On January 5th, 1961, Dr. Timothy Leary, on the advice of Allen Ginsberg, wrote to Burroughs and requested his expert help in testing out an hallucinogenic mushroom. He outlined the scientific nature of the study, and talked about the experiment as an important step in freeing this potentially mind-expanding substance from social control... Of course, he was speaking Burroughs' language, and later that month Burroughs replied in the affirmative, using language not unlike that used by L. Ron Hubbard, and clearly making reference to Scientology's auditing process: "I think the wider use of these drugs would lead to better conditions at all levels. Perhaps whole areas of neurosis could be mapped and eradicated in mass therapy."

However, despite his initial enthusiasm, when Burroughs tried psilocybin mushrooms in Paris, in March, he was grossly put off by the visions he suffered. In April he returned to Tangier for a short visit, and tried another hallucinogen, Prestonin, which also gave him an unpleasant trip. When Leary arrived in Tangier, he took mushrooms again, but complained that they caused "purple fire... [in] the pain banks," referring to his reactive mind. Although he was convinced that hallucinogens were not for him, it was following his Prestonin trip that Burroughs started performing cut-ups with photographs, laying out his pictures with random objects and taking photographs of the photographs.

When Ginsberg met Burroughs in Tangier, it was their first meeting since the Beat Hotel back in 1958. Burroughs had changed a great deal since then. He had – to use a Reichian term – put on a lot of character armor. Since writing *Naked Lunch* he had become more guarded. He was also firmly under the influence of Gysin, who Ginsberg disliked. Ginsberg also disliked the Cut-up Method, as he felt Burroughs' writing was already lacking in linear narrative, and failed to see the value in chopping it up further. He felt Burroughs was attempted to cut up the world around him, breaking everything down in his paranoia, and becoming totally inhuman. When they met for the first time in years, Burroughs snapped, "Who are you an agent for?" and accused Ginsberg of being overly influenced by figures of authority from his past. Whilst Ginsberg could not entirely refute this, it was proof that Burroughs was indeed cutting up everything he saw – even his friends. His interests in Scientology and anthropology had come together to create an even colder and more detached view of the world.

Despite their disagreements, Leary offered to fly Burroughs out to Boston to further participate in studies on hallucinogens. Burroughs, however, went along but became increasingly unimpressed by Leary's operation. In particular, he felt it was totally lacking in scientific merit. "They had utterly no interest in any scientific work," he complained. Burroughs wanted to talk about computers and brain functions, but Leary and his friends wanted to trip, and to get other people to trip. According to Burroughs, after refusing to jump on board the psychedelic bandwagon, Leary withdrew funding and Burroughs was left with the bill for his flights to and from America.

Angered with Leary, Burroughs took a cheap apartment in Brooklyn, and began work on the final book in what was to become in his Nova Trilogy, *Nova Express*. Although it wasn't published until 1964, Burroughs appears to have more or less finished the book by early 1962. In January excerpts were published in Evergreen, and by April he claims to have finished the project and delivered it to the publishers, even before the second book in the trilogy, *The Ticket That Exploded*, was written. Burroughs later explained that, "In *Naked Lunch* and *The Soft Machine* I have diagnosed an illness, and in *The Ticket That Exploded* and *Nova Express* is suggested a remedy."

In February Burroughs returned to London and was saddened to learn of the death of Kells Elvins, the man who had on several occasions pushed him into writing, most notably giving him the idea for *Junky*. Their first story together, "Twilight's Last Gleaming," was used almost verbatim in *Nova Express*.

Burroughs quickly set about writing *The Ticket That Exploded*, and in March *Naked Lunch* went on sale in the U.S. At some point Burroughs also found the time to rewrite *The Soft Machine* for its next edition.

Burroughs' first ever interview was recorded that year by Ginsberg and Corso. It provides an early glimpse of his views that remained fairly steady over the coming decade. He begins by restating his old factualism theory: "To concern yourself with surface political conflicts is to make the mistake of the bull in the ring, you are charging the cloth." Corso proves provocative and insightful, continually pushing Burroughs, who sometimes talks himself into corners without realizing or acknowledging the fact. He makes the suggestion, which frequently appears in his work, that humans should avoid thinking in words, and instead create an alternate language of pictures or colors. When Burroughs explains the Cut-up Method, Corso poses the question that numerous critics have posed: just how can you use language to inform people that they shouldn't use language. Burroughs doesn't have an answer: "Precisely what I was saying — if you talk you always end up with politics, it gets nowhere. I mean man it's strictly from the soft typewriter." Throughout, Burroughs pretty much states in more precise terms the key ideas from *The Soft Machine*.

In April Burroughs wrote Gysin that he had experimented with audio cut-ups, using Gysin's phrase "I AM THAT I AM," the permutations of which Gysin had released on BBC radio to the second lowest audience approval in history. Burroughs was impressed that it sounded like "Mayan" when played backwards. He also cut it up in a more traditional way, at least by his standards. "I went to the Hubbard Center and picked up some literature and cut I AM WHAT I AM into it with various other suggestions verbal and musical backwards and forwards speed it up slow it down." Here he is referring to the November trip to the nearby Scientology center, where he smuggled out the Preclear Assessment Sheets, and possibly some other documents. In an undated cut-up called "Some Phrases From Scientology Procedures Cut-in", which Burroughs filed alongside numerous cut-ups from between 1960 and 1972, we quite possibly have a transcript of this effort. Certainly it contains both Scientology materials and parts of Gysin's "I AM THAT I AM" work. It begins:

> "I am nobody I am every body I am me I am
> you I am myself I am others it was your idea
> but not mine shook hands without enthusiasm
> looked sullenly at the floor turned abruptly
> away lighting a cigarette far flung organization
> ruthless agents unlimited funds you may not
> realize the importance of the Chinese preliminary
> experiments lost voice whispering…"

Throughout this text Burroughs makes frequent errors in typing. Most likely he was speed-typing in order to transcribe the recording, providing further evidence that this is indeed the cut-up to which he referred in his letter to Gysin. He wrote to Gysin that it included Scientology materials cut with Gysin's writing and unspecified other work, but it is clear from some references that Burroughs was including his own writing. Determining which words exactly came from which text is tricky. The repetition of "I" and "am" of course suggests Gysin's, and below we see unmistakable references to Burroughs' childhood, but picking out the ones from Scientology pamphlets is tough. Hubbard used colloquial language to express his ideas, and as part of auditing it was common to use simple phrases on any topic. For example, the first question, as taken from a bulletin in 1964 (although used before then), would be: "Tell me what you are willing to talk about." The use of the word "Chinese," however, likely came from Hubbard, who despised the Chinese, as well as "agent" which was often used in his work as both verb and noun.

> "…I have no words left breathing old pulp
> magazines I dust off the dead Gods lonely fringes
> of a remote next stop spit blood at dawn the old

broken point of origin St. Louis Missouri smell
of sickness in the room..."

The cut-up is messy and pure, with nothing appearing to be left out, and no grammar forced upon it. In the summer, Burroughs would mention in a letter that he had gone back to his original views and had stopped being selective with his cut-ups, saying, "I can often transcribe whole passages verbatim." This one appears to have come straight from the tape recorder – as though by the voices Burroughs heard when "transcribing" *Naked Lunch* - and provides a fascinating glimpse into the author's mind. Clearly from the reference to his hometown we can see that Burroughs has cut in some of his own work.[10] Interestingly, we also have reference to "old pulp magazines." Burroughs enjoyed reading these as a child, and the dark tone throughout the piece shows his lament for a lost childhood. The last line is particularly haunting: "far away toys spirits of the night."

This cut-up went unpublished, which is sad given its success. Despite being as pure as a cut-up could be, it is filled with meaning and in parts even sounds poetic. It comes as close as any cut-up Burroughs published to cutting into the truth – perhaps, ironically, the truth about Burroughs himself. This validates Burroughs' interpretation of cut-ups as a form of auditing.

Burroughs' visit to the Scientology headquarters was not simply a means of obtaining material to subject to the Cut-up Method. Shortly after this visit he began taking Scientology classes, and wrote a series of short essays that demonstrate his progress. The first was a short hand-written essay entitled "Security Checking Fundamentals." It goes far beyond the information outlined in Hubbard's *Dianetics*, and shows Burroughs starting to take his studies seriously, even using some of Hubbard's own jargon.

"He withholds to avoid punishment... The

---

10 "old broken point of origin St. Louis Missouri" appears in *The Wild Boys* and *Exterminator!* It is taken from a book Burroughs read, which inspired *The Wild Boys*, called *The Twilight World* by Poul Anderson. "Spitting blood" or "spit blood" is a phrase that appears in many of Burroughs' books.

> common [handwriting unclear] between the P.C.
> and the reactive mind is the withheld. The pulling
> of withelds is the first step towards getting the
> P.C. to take control of the reactive mind...
> We are processing the individual up towards
> Knowingness. In the church the auditor must look
> at a question on the meter until P.C. has reached
> an impasse.
> "A man with overts will not clear a withheld is a
> no motion often a dangerous and floats in Time
> due to the action of the overts."[11]

In this essay, Burroughs demonstrates an increasing awareness of Scientology ideas, and his use of their jargon indicates that his reading has gone further than just that of their security checking methods. Although Hubbard's *Dianetics* was deliberately accessible, and in it he states the barrier language poses to understanding, the literature distributed among Scientologists in the early 1960s could be quite complicated. Hubbard continued to use colloquial language, but as the material increased with the member's progression through the religion, the ideas and jargon became more complex. To understand the material that Burroughs was describing, and to use the jargon that he used, he would most likely have done a lot of preliminary reading.

Evidently, Burroughs viewed the use of language by Hubbard as a means of breaking free from convention, and fails to see that organizations (or, as some would put it, cults) frequently make use of language as a means of unifying the group, of convincing members of the power held by the leaders, of controlling the spread of ideas, and of creating an "us and them" divide in order to devalue criticism from outside. Hubbard was a master of thought control through the technique of altering the language of his followers, who later came to think and dream in "Scientologese." In particular he liked to change verbs into

---

11 P.C. – a preclear, or person who is undergoing Scientology auditing.
Withhold/ withheld – a destructive thought that you are hiding from others.
Overt – a sin or crime against the moral code of a group, intentional or
otherwise.

nouns, use abbreviations and acronyms, and to add the suffix "-ness" to the end of words. He also liked to change the meaning of everyday words (as demonstrated even in his most accessible book, *Dianetics*) to what he believed the meaning should be, thereby subverting his followers' use of language to give him control over their speech and thoughts. Members seeking to leave the Church of Scientology have often encountered difficulty in communicating with counselors and family members who are unfamiliar with these new elements of speech, giving the religion additional power over their lives, and making it hard to turn away.

In the summer of 1962, Burroughs was invited to speak at the International Writers' Conference at the Edinburgh Festival. As *Junky* had gone largely unnoticed, and his more recent books had been printed only in small editions (with *Naked Lunch* still not yet available in America or the U.K.), Burroughs was only invited at the last minute, and was required to pay his own way. It was, however, an important event, and his input cemented his reputation as a serious writer, garnering him the support necessary to survive the forthcoming obscenity trials. On the subject of obscenity, Burroughs paraphrased Korzybski and Hubbard, and made reference to Reich. In discussing the future of the novel he talked about Gysin and the Cut-up Method, and also labeled himself "a map-maker, an explorer or psychic areas." He talked about time- and space-travel, and said that in his novels he is "primarily concerned with the question of survival" – another nod to Hubbard.

Upon returning from Edinburgh, Burroughs met Antony Balch, a filmmaker interested in turning some of Burroughs' cut-ups into film. Of course, Burroughs was interested in spreading his ideas to a new medium, and agreed. Together they made *Towers Open Fire*, a short film starring Burroughs alongside Sommerville, Mikey Portman, and Gysin.[12] In it Burroughs reads routines and chants curses over a collection of bizarre images, with disorienting sounds, and references are made to flicker, Egyptian hieroglyphics, and the Cut-up Method. During roughly

12 Portman was a troubled young man who took a liking to Burroughs, and became one of his lovers and a part of his circle for several years.

the same period of time, Balch also filmed Burroughs and his friends for a project that eventually became *The Cut Ups*. It aimed to bring to film what Burroughs had brought to literature, through cutting up the film, and aiming at disorienting the viewer. The film plays scenes at differing speeds, and this appears to be a device suggested by Burroughs, who sent numerous letters to Balch with ideas for film-making. Throughout, Burroughs and Gysin chant phrases from Scientology auditing instructions: "Hello – Yes – Hello - Look at that picture - Does it seem to be persisting? – Good - Thank You." Gysin later claimed that this was his idea, and not Burroughs'. Whilst the film was an example of the Cut-up Method applied to cinema, it also aimed, via repetition of imagery, to achieve the same effects as Gysin's Dream Machine.

Around Christmas *The Ticket That Exploded* was published by Olympia Press. Again, the book was comprised of material from his word hoard, mixed with newer writing. It built upon the ideas set forth in *The Soft Machine*, namely in exploring the use of language as a virus. There are references to all of Burroughs' interests and obsessions at the time: Hassan ibn Sabbah, apomorphine, Reich and orgones, Korzybski, Brion Gysin, tape recorders, nuclear weapons, the Mayans, and the importance of developing non-written, sub-vocal communication. When he later revised the book, Burroughs updated information about the technology and included details about using cameras to create visual cut-ups.

The book references Scientology without subtlety. Burroughs goes to the length of calling the group "the Logos," but then gives the game away by describing them in terms that leaves no doubt over who he really meant:[13]

> "They have a system of therapy they call 'clearing'. You 'run' traumatic material which they call 'engrams' until it loses emotional connotation through repetitions and is then refilled

13 "Logos" is a reference to logocentrism, where "logos" is the ideal representation of an idea or an object in language, as well as to the Greek, "logos," meaning simply "word."

as neutral memory. When all the 'engrams' have
been run and deactivated the subject becomes a
'clear.'"

That Burroughs repeats this one idea from Scientology
highlights the fact that it was his primary interest, and it had
been ever since his introduction by Gysin in 1959. He is being
pretty clear in his opinion that Scientology auditing can be a
huge benefit for humanity, however, he cautions that such a
powerful tool in the fight against control can in turn become a
method of control. He suggests that someone may become clear
by "unloading their 'engram' tapes on somebody else" and hints
that he distrusts the "front men and women" for holding too much
power. Although the latter criticism has been asserted by many
critics of Scientology, the former is more unusual, but something
that Burroughs would continue to fear for many years.

There are also far less obvious references in the text. Burroughs
uses the phrase "Present time," as recommended by Hubbard. He
talks about "havingness" (a common Scientology term), thinking
in identities (Hubbard via Korzybski), language as a negative
stimulus upon the human mind, the importance of silence, and
the sole purpose of humanity as survival. All of these are easily
recognizable to those well-versed in Scientology, but went over
the head of most of Burroughs' readers, and were interpreted as
products of his bizarre imagination.

It may seem odd for a writer, and particularly one who claimed
to have transcribed his most successful work from a voice in his
head, but internal silence greatly appealed to Burroughs. In *The
Ticket That Exploded* he suggests it as a weapon:

> "Modern man has lost the option of silence. Try
> halting your sub-vocal speech. Try to achieve even
> ten seconds of inner silence. You will encounter a
> resisting organism that forces you to talk."

This "resisting organism" is the Dianetic demon, explained
by Hubbard in *Dianetics* as a problem in the wiring between

the reactive and analytic mind. It's not a serious problem, and Hubbard speculates that all aberrees[14] have this "demon circuit" within them, causing them to hear words that that are normally transferred from the memory banks to the conscious part of the brain silently. Naturally, a clear does not suffer from demons.

However, Burroughs retained a little skepticism regarding the importance of silence. He was keen to destroy the demon inside him, and to protect himself from its pernicious influence, but it was also the voices in his head that gave him material as a writer. In *Naked Lunch* he wrote about the "cured writer" who is no longer able to write because his interest in Buddhism has caused him to stop thinking in terms of words. Burroughs had been interested, at times, in Buddhism, which also stressed the value of sub-vocal speech, but again he worried about the results of removing inner voices with meditation, later connecting this to Scientology:

> "When Huxley got Buddhism, he stopped writing novels and wrote Buddhist tracts. Meditation, astral travel, telepathy, are all a means to an end for a novelist. I even got copy out of scientology. It's a question of emphasis. Any writer who does not consider his writing the most important thing he does, who does not consider writing his only salvation, I – 'I trust him little in the commerce of the soul.'"

Following his appearance at the Edinburgh Festival, Burroughs' *Naked Lunch* was now selling well, and was finally available in the United States courtesy of Grove Press. However, in January the police arrested the owner of a Boston bookstore for selling it, and a court date was set for two years later, on which date it would be decided whether or not Burroughs' book was obscene. In the meantime Burroughs was left wanting for cash, having presumptuously told his parents that he no longer needed their financial support, now that he'd made it as an internationally renowned author.

14 Aberree – a person with aberrations, ie not yet clear

In February, 1963, Burroughs wrote "Cut Up with Scientology lit," which appears to be a mixture of Scientology materials and his own notes of having been audited at the local Scientology center. The tone of this piece is unusually lighthearted, and he talks about eating peanuts and drinking Pepsi during a break in auditing. Typically Burroughs' cut-ups are permeated with darkness as he attempts to cut to the brutal cold facts behind a piece of writing, but here everything is happy. There are the usual terms of Scientologese – "GPM," "2-I2A," "R2," "I2," "3MA," etc – but much of the text is surprisingly coherent. It goes from vague statements about the Church - "We sure have the technology. All we have to do is learn and use it." - to ruminations on unspecified moments of pleasure – "It was very nice. Sort of cool and clean." He mentions Mary Sue Hubbard (L. Ron's wife), indicating that perhaps she was his auditor, although no mention of this fact is made anywhere else in his writing.

It's easy to forget that Burroughs had a son. Billy, who'd been sent to live with his grandparents after Burroughs shot Joan in 1951, grew up "cursed." He felt he was doomed to live in his father's footsteps, and this feeling resulted in a nervous breakdown when he was only fifteen years old, after accidentally shooting his friend in the neck with his .22 rifle. It was only the latest in a long line of troubles for the young boy, and it was decided that the following year, after his sixteenth birthday, he would join his father in Tangier. The two had rarely spent time together, although Burroughs sent his son presents and letters over the years.

In the summer of 1963, Burroughs moved from London to Tangier with his two lovers, Portman and Ian Sommerville, and they all moved into a house with his son, Billy. Burroughs introduced Billy to marijuana, took him to gay bars, and allowed him to sleep on a sofa in the midst of the usual Tangier excess. He was groped and molested and quickly came to hate the place. The two couldn't communicate, and over the six months that they were together their relationship deteriorated to the point that they decided Billy should return to Palm Beach and his grandparents. Burroughs had hoped that they would be able to share some sort of emotion – be it crying or screaming in anger – but there was nothing there. It was just like the relationship between Burroughs and his own father, Mortimer. He blamed himself. He had made a late attempt at being a parent, and had failed miserably.

In late summer and fall, Burroughs was still studying Scientology. On August 4th he wrote himself a summary of Hubbard's recent literature on the E-meter, called "E Meter Errors-Comm Cycle Error."[15] Again, he makes liberal use of Hubbard's jargon and acronyms. In this case, Burroughs is studying the finer points of E-meter use, and makes notes on how to get results and avoid mistakes in auditing. Most of his notes revolve around the idea of "tonearm," or "TA," referring to a part of the E-meter whose action indicates success in auditing. "Don't demand more than the P.C. can tell you," he says. "Don't receive less than the P.C. has to say." He also alludes to the difference between "whatsit" and "itsa." In Hubbard's guidelines, he states that a preclear will advance quickly in Scientology if he can focus on what something is ("itsa"), whereas if he dwells on what he does not know, and has to ask questions ("whatsit"), he will get bogged down and make little progress. Burroughs notes, "The rise of Ta 'Whatsit?' – the fall is 'itsa.'" In Hubbard's description, "itsa" indicates an awareness of "facts" and an ability to observe and process information, whereas the opposite results in "non-facts," which cause confusion. No doubt this appealed to the founder of Factualism, who once wrote that "madness is confusion of levels of fact."

Two days later, Burroughs wrote another short essay, focusing on "Auditing and Comm Cycles." This time he lays on the jargon even heavier than before, and understanding what he means requires pretty extensive research into Scientology. He begins: "The Auditor is restimulating the pc. Auditor must not stop because of restimulated somatics." Here, "restimulate" means to turn on an unpleasant memory, and "somatics" are the

15 Comm[unication] cycle – in auditing, Hubbard laid out a strict system for communication between the auditor and the preclear, with a definite start and end, hence "cycle."

physical pains that come with traumatic memories. From Reich, Burroughs already had the idea that illness could be caused by society, and from there it is only a short leap to the notion of words causing illness, or physical pain. Again, this demonstrates that his primary interest in Scientology related to the impact of memories. Then he poses the question, "Do birds fly?" and speculates at the result: "This causes a picture of birds and a query of the picture. Are they flying? You are listening to inside of skull which is least important and also hardest to detect when it isn't being done." Burroughs equates this to his old passion, "telepathy."

A month later, another essay explores his interpretations of "Repetitive Rudiments," referring to a period prior to each auditing session during which time a preclear must divulge his or her problems. It seems, once again, that Burroughs is taking his studies seriously, demonstrating a lot of knowledge. However, he appears to still be lacking any form of critical thinking, and the skepticism he first inherited from Gysin had faded over the past few years. Perhaps the Scientology literature was too persuasive for him, or perhaps he had simply found what he wanted. Burroughs describes the process of running rudiments (also known as "ruds"): "1) Run rud as a repetitive process until p.c. has no answer. 2) consult meter for a hidden answer. 3) If meter reads use it to steer… the pc to the answer." All this sounds terribly controlling, and yet there is not a hint of criticism in his notes at this point, nor any negative commentary in his correspondence. He appears entirely enamored by his newfound beliefs, suggesting that from his first encounter in 1959, his enthusiasm had not only failed to wane, but was growing as he learned more and more.

In November, 1963, John Calder put out a "safe" collection of Burroughs' work – *Dead Fingers Talk*. The book contained heavily edited excerpts of all Burroughs' Olympia Press titles – *Naked Lunch*, *The Soft Machine*, and *The Ticket That Exploded*. Given the origin of the material and Burroughs' propensity for cutting up and revising his work, it's not surprising to sometimes see it listed as one of his novels, rather than a reader or collection.

It was also unusual in that it was printed as a hardback, as Burroughs' work was typically paperback only, but it was again printed as a small run, as Calder didn't expect the book to be a big seller. It created quite a stir, however, with a famous battle playing out on the pages of the *Times Literary Supplement* for thirteen weeks after the book's publication, and paved the way for Calder to put out a UK edition of *Naked Lunch* the following year. In December, Lawrence Ferlinghetti's City Lights published *The Yagé Letters*, Burroughs' collaboration with Allen Ginsberg, featuring correspondence from their South American travels.

At the start of 1964, Burroughs was depressed by his failure at parenthood, more troubles with obtaining royalties from Olympia Press, and by learning that he was no longer particularly welcome in the U.K. On a trip to London for a TV interview, he was told that his usual visa conditions were no longer applicable, presumably due to his increasing notoriety. He was stuck in Tangier for most of the next year, where anti-foreigner hostility made life unpleasant.

In March he wrote another short essay, "Auditing and Assessment," showing that despite the ups and downs in his life, and the changes in location, he was nonetheless keeping up with his studies in Scientology. More than ever he sounds like L. Ron Hubbard – adopting terms of Scientologese and using a similar style of writing. However, at times he also rambles into stream-of-consciousness nonsense. It starts, for no apparent reason, "I've seen some creeps disappear since last time I looked at You," before getting into the differences between assessing and auditing. By this point, Burroughs is studying techniques associated with Level VII, a fairly advanced stage of study. In a fairly straightforward passage, he says:

> "Auditor is going to assess so he begins the assess[ment] by addressing PC. This is an auditing action. He must complete auditing cycle before assessing. If he does not the assess will be defeated."

Again, Burroughs is focusing on the auditing process, demonstrating admirable progress and showing a knack for the language. These short essays – never published – highlight his desire to master not just the basics of Scientology, but to be able to perform auditing at all levels.

Only three months later, on June 18th, he wrote a longer essay, this time veering away from Hubbard's style of writing and back to a more familiar one, although he continues to use some Scientology vocabulary. Here it appears he is suffering some from some doubts. The essay is simply titled "Study," and is composed oddly – with handwritten time-stamps on the far left of the page, and what appear to be page numbers running on the inside left of his commentary. It seems that Burroughs was studying some unnamed material when he became disaffected and began an unstructured musing on Hubbard and his methods.

> "If an auditor can't learn he can't audit so the subject is application of tech. Ron's course in salesmanship all kinds of methods of flagar[ant] theft tech 1910 way. Only one went forward and the other techs are lost… Dead or lost techs.
>
> "They lose the pieces. Tech is lost because people can't study. They must be evolution subject studied. The chemical committed pages to memory. The gate is willingness to know. Scientology has the discipline of how you do it. Auditory discipline, handling the meter, the comm cycle. It is application that could get lost… Learn the subject of auditing not just a few processes. The auditing command won't arrive unless you do it right.
>
> "Photography, aztecs, chemistry. He fear he know all about it, so why study it? He not willing to learn a few tricks."

Although it's difficult to follow and to ascertain his exact meaning, Burroughs' tone appears dark. He appears to be questioning Hubbard, which he would continue to do in the future. He refers disparagingly to him as "Ron" and to Scientology as "salesmanship" and suggests that Dianetics was pieced together from old bits of wisdom and science. Indeed, Burroughs would have been more than aware of the origins of some of Hubbard's ideas, and it's not unfair to suggest that his books owed a debt to many unnamed thinkers before him. It is also unclear what he means by the loss of technology, but more than likely he was referring to the fact that Hubbard ultimately determined what his followers learned. If he picked and chose from the technology and information before him, who's to say that there wasn't more there that he left behind? Moreover, Hubbard was never willing to open his methods to the scrutiny of the scientific community, and to Burroughs that was always a tremendous failure. Perhaps he was afraid Hubbard's advances would be lost because of being kept secret.

Another interpretation is that the repetition of "can't learn" and "can't study" could simply refer to Burroughs himself. He was in a depressed mood much of that year, and if he was unable to focus and study as he wanted, he might have feared that he was stalling or reversing in his drive to better understand Scientology. Perhaps he is addressing himself when he says, "Learn the subject of auditing not just a few processes." Throughout his life, Burroughs developed a number of obsessions and whilst these were important to him, it could be argued that he never fully gave himself over to any of them except the Cut-up Method. He seemed to be aware of his disorganized approach to, for example, his South American adventures, and perhaps he was aware that his research into Scientology was becoming sporadic. He might have felt as though he was focusing too much on one or two "processes" rather than learning the whole thing.

Either way, it is evident from a close reading of the middle of the above quote that he still felt strongly about the potential held in Hubbard's ideas: "Scientology has the discipline of how you do it. Auditory discipline, handling the meter, the comm cycle." Clearly his views on the auditing procedure, particularly learning to listen and detect truth from behind speech (in essence, cutting-up a preclear's answers), were still very positive.

1964 also saw the publication of the final installment of Burroughs' Nova Trilogy, *Nova Express*, the book he considered to be his "clearest statement" of his opinions and goals. Certainly his assault on language is more overt. The book can been seen in some ways as closer to a conventional narrative, with definite good guys and bad guys, and the bad guys are space invaders whose weapon of choice is mind control. This is achieved, of course, by manipulating and taking control of language. It is at the same time a manifesto as much as a novel. One can consider it a sort of refresher course on the lessons given in *The Soft Machine* and *The Ticket That Exploded*. Burroughs is explicit in his messages, and the book turns into lectures at points, with his narrator, William Lee, saying things like, "The purpose of my writing is to expose and arrest Nova Criminals..." and offering defenses for his (Burroughs') other novels. He uses extensive footnotes perhaps as a new extension of the Cut-up Method, where there are two narratives going on – one in the text and one in the footnote, that the reader unintentionally cut together. These footnotes are written in an entirely coherent style, too, offering the reader supposedly scientific and impartial evidence to support the main body of text.

Nova Express is littered with references to the obsessions that have dominated the author's life, and which he viewed as weapons in the war against these alien invaders. There is Reich and his orgone theory ("Martin is stealing *your orgones*. – You going to stand still for this shit?"), Dr. Dent's apomorphine treatment ("You can cut the enemy off your line by the judicious use of apomorphine and silence – *Use the sanity drug apomorphine.*"), Hassan ibn Sabbah (" *'Nothing Is True – Everything Is Permitted'* – *Last Words Hassan I Sabbah*"), Jack Black (" And you can see the marks are wising up, standing around in sullen groups and that mutter gets louder and louder."), Mayans and Aztecs ("you will regret calling in the Mayan Aztec Gods with your synthetic mushrooms."), Brion Gysin ("Preliminary reports indicate that certain painting – like Brion Gysin's – when projected on a subject produced some of the effects observed in orgone accumulators

-"), flicker ("goofed on ether and mixed in flicker helmets"), and the atom bomb ("Mobilized reasons to love Hiroshima and Nagasaki?").

Of course, there are numerous references to Scientology, to which refers by its real name, and also the name "Logos," which he used in *The Ticket That Exploded*:

> "Scientology means the study of 'humanity's condition' – Wise radio doctor- Logos Officers in his portable – The Effects Boy's 'scientology release' is locks over the Chinese – Told me to sit by Hubbard guide – 'What are you going to do? – That person going to get out of 'havingness?'"

A little later, a more intelligible conversation takes place, with a Nova Police cadet explaining the concept of Scientology, which is "part of our Basic Scientology Police Course":

> "The Scientologists believe sir that words recorded during a period of unconsciousness... *store* pain and that this pain store can be lugged in with key words represented as an alternate mathematical formulae indicating number of exposures to the key words and reaction index... they call these words recorded during unconsciousness *engrams* sir... If I may say so sir the childhood amnesia for trauma is of special interest sir... The child *forgets* sir but since the controllers have the engram tapes sir any childhood trauma can be plugged in at any time... The pain that overwhelms that person is basic basic sir and when *basic basic* is wiped off the tape... then that person becomes what they call *clear* sir."

Both of the above quotes come from the same chapter in the novel, "Simple as a Hiccup," which contains numerous references to Scientology. Burroughs often cut his own writing with text from other sources, and so it is possible that he cut some Scientology literature into this part of the novel. Certain words and phrases in densely cut-up passages suggest that he might have: "stimuli," "pain bank," "Present Time," "beingness," "process," "barriers," "purposes," "pre-clear," "no effect," "cycle of action," "identities," "real is real," "reality need," etc. Of particular interest is the reference in the middle of the second quote to childhood traumas and their ability to crop up again in later life and cause pain. Burroughs also describes, with the aid of a Dr. Benway-style hospital routine, how even under anesthesia a person can remember absolutely everything around him – a point of which Hubbard was certain. The message is clear – if Scientology can erase these foul scars from the mind, it is an invaluable tool.

Although the chapter is seemingly unintelligible, Scientology is presented as a "simple" solution to the pain and suffering the world wrought by the forces of control. Horrendous images of medical procedures are presented, but always there's the possibility of erasing the tapes and going back to a place where these memories don't exist. In fact, this view permeates the whole of the book – nostalgia for something that never existed. Burroughs harkens back to a sort of Eden that existed before the atom bomb, and in this particular chapter that Eden is equated with a clear mind – that is to say, one free from engrams. Thus Scientology is the best weapon against the Nova Mob, and a method of travelling back to a more pleasant place in time.

In an interview with Eric Mottram, Burroughs attempted to describe the "mythology" of his work, and in doing so, invokes a number of phrases and ideas that point to his interest in Scientology at the time:

> "Heaven and hell exist in my mythology. Hell consists of falling into enemy hands, into the hands of virus power, and heaven consists of freeing oneself of this power or achieving inner freedom, freedom from conditioning."

He goes on to add that none of the characters in his novels have achieved total freedom precisely because they are part of his novels, and therefore in a "cycle of conditioned action."

Burroughs returned to the United States shortly before Christmas and sat down for an interview with Conrad Knickerbocker of the *Paris Review* on New Year's Day. The interview is frequently cited as one in which Burroughs is on top form, and elaborates quite clearly on a number of issues relating to his work. He talks at ease about the usual subjects: apomorphine, the Cut-up Method, mind control, language as a virus, time travel, and the Mayans. Near the end, Knickerbocker refers to Zen and Reich as "exotic systems," and flatly asks why Burroughs is interested in such nonsense. He replies: "Well, these nonconventional theories frequently touch on something going on that Harvard and MIT can't explain." Knickerbocker follows up by asking about Scientology, obviously implying that it's another of Burroughs' silly interests. Burroughs' answer is surprising:

> "I'm not very interested in such a crudely three-dimensional manipulative schema as L. Ron Hubbard's, although it's got its points. I've studied it and I've seen how it works. It's a series of manipulative gimmicks. They tell you to look around and see what you would have. The results are much more subtle and more successful than Dale Carnegie's."[16]

Although he seemed to express doubts about Hubbard and Scientology in his "Study" essay from the previous summer, and had no doubt been appraised of the movement's negative attributes by Gysin, it is nonetheless odd to hear him speak openly in a critical manner, as up until this point Burroughs seemed more interested in turning people onto Scientology. He clearly believed that Hubbard's ideas – that is to say, Dianetics – were

16 Dale Carnegie was another Missourian, and an extremely successful self-help author, whose most famous work was *How to Win Friends and Influence People*.

of immense importance. However, he appears to be shunning the system, as perhaps he was beginning to view Scientology as just another method of control. Throughout the interview he touts his usual views, whilst being careful not to endorse anything wholeheartedly.

Later in the month, his father died of a heart attack, and Burroughs attended the funeral in Palm Beach. He spent a short time in St. Louis, visiting the woods where the incident with his nanny had occurred, but then settled in New York. The obscenity trial for *Naked Lunch* was going on up in Boston, but he chose not to attend. Soon Burroughs found himself at the center of a subculture. Here was this infamous author, whose now legendary book was on trial in Boston, being defended by Norman Mailer and Allen Ginsberg, giving readings at hip parties. Kids were turning up with copies of his books that they wanted autographed, and Burroughs was adored. Just like the old days in New York he was revered as the wise old man, a mentor to a new generation of young hipsters.

It was a creative year for Burroughs, who was surprised to find himself happy and inspired in New York. His goal was the spread of his ideas, and for the latter half of the decade he would focus on small-press publications, rather than book-length material. He put together a cut-up collage of *Time* magazine to signal his distrust of the *Time-Life* media empire, wrote a lot of what would eventually become *The Third Mind*, and even cut his first LP, *Call Me Burroughs*, with his inimitable voice drawling through some classic routines. In the early sixties, small presses began their rise and Burroughs was constantly sending out material from his word hoard to any editor kind enough to ask. In 1965 he even put out his own publication, called *APO-33 Bulletin: A Metabolic Regulator*.[17] The magazine, whose printing was halted after a technical malfunction, and saw wider release with later editions starting in 1966, begins with Burroughs' "Apomorphine Statement 1." Despite his apparent distrust of the man, the essay starts with a quote from L. Ron Hubbard: "If you wish to hide something it is simply necessary

17 The title is, of course, a reference to apomorphine, a form of metabolic regulation.

to create disinterest in the area where it is hidden." Burroughs goes on to explain that Hubbard "knows more than any man living about the use of word combos to produce certain effects." This is a monumentally important statement, and was repeated in Burroughs' column for Jeff Nuttall's influential publication, *My Own Mag*. For Burroughs during this period, fighting control mechanisms was the only important battle, and although his works allude to the significance of Scientology (in conjunction with other forces) in fighting this control, this statement sums up his views perfectly.

In December Burroughs wrote Balch with the intention of producing a new type of science fiction movie – with Scientology's methods used as a weapon, and also with the religion as a sort of sci-fi bad guy. "The story is the story of scientology and their attempt to take over the planet," he says. He goes on to describe a part of the film:

> "Take 1: a shabby street as we move up the street we see a sign 'YOU can use this phone'... Now we pan in on the doorway over which is written... 'Come in. We are friends of yours'... The man behind the camera is obviously standing in front of the building deciding whether or not to go in... A figure of indeterminate sex appears in the doorway with a smile of welcome... "Come in friend," the camera starts forward. 'What do you want? Get out!' the camera recoils... The sign changes to 'Members only.' Switch back and forth the camera advancing and recoiling. Finally the figure in the doorway is smiling welcome from one side of its face and spitting hate from the other faster and faster until it fuzzs out of focus..."

"Take 2" is a lecture, with a female Scientologist demonstrating the power of opposing phrases, such as "I love you, I hate you," "Yes, no," and also using the "Hello – Yes – Hello" routine in which Burroughs had long since shown some interest. The audience repeats these phrases, which are recorded and played back.

The movie sounds vaguely similar to some of the threads running through the Nova Trilogy, and in particular *The Soft Machine*. When Burroughs says that "your planet has been invaded and the landing field for this invasion was precisely the human body," he evokes the idea of humans as tape recorders and words as controlling commands. However, it appears that now, rather than a method for resisting the invasion, Scientology is part of it – they are the ones issuing the commands. The letter demonstrates a wariness of Scientology that is often lacking in his work, and in particular a keen eye for the process of luring people in, only to find secrecy.

It appears that during 1965, Burroughs' infatuation with Scientology had waned. Although his faith in their methods stood strong, he was becoming more paranoid and distrustful, and was starting to view Scientology as an organization rather than a philosophy. He was becoming aware of its negative qualities. In a letter later in the month, he compared it to Communism, Mayan priests, the *Time-Life* empire, and the Catholic Church as a means of control. He accuses them of attempting to gain a spiritual monopoly, saying that they are as bad as any other organization in their unwillingness to contemplate the possibility of another way.

Still, Burroughs was not entirely dissuaded, and the following year, in February, he was sending Scientology literature to Gysin, the very same man who had years before introduced Burroughs to Scientology.

Despite his fame and productivity, Burroughs missed Sommerville and London, and claimed that America was "a bore. Nothing here really. I just stay in my loft and work." By September he was back in the U.K. At immigration he was only granted a month-long visa, but he later had it extended to three months. That meant Burroughs had to leave the country by Christmas, and so he spent the holidays in Tangier. Burroughs moved back to London in January 1966, but Sommerville had taken up with a new man, and Burroughs was depressed. In July, though, *Naked Lunch* was finally judged not obscene, and things were looking positive, at least in a financial success. Despite his fame, having his book banned had made it difficult for Burroughs to actually receive any royalties, and his letters from this period are filled with complaints about the situation. With his royalties finally coming through, he was even able to help out his mother, who was struggling after the death of Mortimer.

Burroughs' opinions on Scientology throughout early 1966 indicate that his obsession was nearing an end. He wrote, in a letter to Gysin, about his dislike of the group's leader:

> "I am not sorry to see L. Ron Hubbard in hot water. *The Sunday People* local scandal sheet here wrote him up a full page spread… the article says he is full of venom and is sending out paid spies to smear anyone who opposes scientology with the idea of causing them legal trouble, one assumes through paid informers as well. I would suggest they check his tax payments and his right to call St Hill an educational institution."[18]

Yet he was still drawn to its ideas, as they related so strongly to other views that he held. His interest in tape recorders showed no sign of abating, and in early 1966 he was using them to record audio cut-ups. At the center of this was the phrase, "Hello – Yes – Hello," which on at least one occasion Burroughs played outside the Scientology headquarters. The purpose of such acts for Burroughs was usually destructive: "The mere act of playing a street recording back in the street makes a hole in reality." Together with Antony Balch, he took videos of the same building and set them to a soundtrack of fire engines and bombs exploding, with the same intended purpose.

His obsession with tape recorders would continue to grow over the coming years, but in November, 1966, he published an essay

18 In the mid-sixties, Hubbard and Scientology were under attack from newspapers around the world, and reports about Hubbard's finances and questionable practices were common.

called "Invisible Generation" in the counterculture newspaper, *International Times*. The opening line, which Burroughs repeated in several of his letters during the latter half of that year, read: "what we see is determined to a large extent by what we hear." This essay described how to use tape recorders as a revolutionary weapon, and Burroughs frequently cited it in other essays over the coming decade. In a letter just after publication of "Invisible Generation," Burroughs commented that there was an advertisement for the Church of Scientology on the back page, "saying very much what I say in my article." It read:

> **"hubbard scientology organisation in london**: Scientology can help anyone handle and change the conditions of his life and environment. You are invited to a free introductory lecture every weekday evening at 7pm. 37 Fitzroy Street, London. W.1. LAN."

It's unclear exactly what part of that tiny classified ad Burroughs was referring to, but he had always associated Scientology closely with tape recorders and cut-ups. He once expressed a great deal of surprise that Hubbard had not included any mention of tape recorders in his books, and investigated further, finding a distributor that claimed to have sold two machines to Hubbard. He claimed that Sommerville, whose opinion of Scientology was unchanged, became ill at the thought of the old conman in possession of such expensive recording equipment.

In September Billy Jr. told his grandmother that he was going camping, but instead hitchhiked to New York and got himself arrested for possession of amphetamines. He'd developed a drug problem after being sent to a boarding school for troubled children, and he was becoming reckless. He called Allen Ginsberg, who bailed him out and got a lawyer to have the charge overturned on the grounds of an illegal search, but soon after, Billy was arrested again on the same charge. Again, Ginsberg came to the rescue, and had the charges overturned. He wrote Burroughs saying that he wanted "to become able to understand my father."

Billy clearly needed his father, but Burroughs was reluctant to help. Billy's behavior was killing his grandmother and driving everyone else to distraction, but Burroughs was back on junk again and didn't want to deal with the flight to America. It was Christmas before he did the right thing, and soon found himself in the middle of the family responsibility that he'd shirked for years. Laura was hallucinating and needed taken to the hospital, and Billy was out of control. In February of 1967, Burroughs checked his son into the same Lexington rehab clinic where he'd spent time after his own first bust in New York.

Around Christmas, Burroughs was again questioning Scientology. In a letter from Palm Beach to Gysin, he compares to L. Ron Hubbard to a Catholic priest ("we know how evil an old priest can be"), refers to Hubbard and the Cookes as "fakers with super human pretentions based on a few simple tricks," and calls Scientology a "shameless fraud." He goes on to question the very notion of an engram, which was something in which he'd always had a great deal of faith:

> "L. Ron Hubbard has stated that words or sounds are recorded by an unconscious subject that these words which he calls engrams in deep sleep have not, to the best of my knowledge, been exposed to words and sounds and then checked to see if these words and sounds elicit any special reaction when the subject is conscious. Assuming that his assumption is correct, what would characterize *all* engrams? Since the photographic mechanism is unquestionably out of action *engrams are characterized by the absence of image.*"

He returned to London in March and started writing his next novel, *The Wild Boys*, but found it difficult with Sommerville and Portman hanging around. He complained about the police presence and a crackdown on narcotics following the famous drug bust at Keith Richards' Redlands manor in Sussex. "I suspect the scientologists stirred all this up," he told Gysin. He then claimed that the Church was about to be banned from the United Kingdom, and said it would be the "best thing [that] ever happened." In fact, Burroughs was plotting against the Church of Scientology, and planned to write an article making his views public. His comments clearly indicate that he had been reading extensively from British tabloid newspapers:

> "My latest piece in which I bluntly accuse L. Ron Hubbard of clearing his wretched clears by dumping their engram garbage in the streets may result in legal action from Hubbard — he is litigation prone I understand. However he is *persona* not altogether *grata* in England has been asked to leave Rhodesia and Australia as a menace to public health and accused in the press of using his so-called therapy as an instrument of blackmail, so I doubt if he would risk a trial and the disclosures that might ensue. In the same article I have attacked *Encounter Magazine* — they admit receiving money from the CIA — as an equal menace to public health. In fact the policies and aims of L. Ron Hubbard are so consistent with the policies and aims of the CIA American Narcotics Dept Institute for Cultural Freedom — also admittedly subsidized — that he may well have been subsidized himself. No I don't think he would risk a public airing of his financial arrangements."

However, despite his talk, it would be almost two years before he published any sort of scathing essay about Hubbard or Scientology.

Tired of England, he soon moved to Marrakesh in order to have the space to write. From there he moved back to Tangier in June, before returning to London. He continued to send checks to his son, but as always his brother, Mort, was still stuck dealing with the harsh realities of family life as Burroughs bounced around the world. Their mother, Laura, was getting sick and could no longer take care of herself. That summer, Billy took up with a girl called Karen and decided to get married, threatening to make Burroughs a grandfather.

In London, Burroughs was becoming "more extreme," in the words of Barry Miles. He was becoming more interested in curses, developing disturbing theories about women (he was beginning to view them as an extraterrestrial phenomenon), and attempting to contact beings on other planets via telepathy. Under Gysin's influence, he had certainly changed a great deal, and by the mid-sixties his usual interest in fringe science had given way to the outright weird. For one thing, he had developed an obsession with the number twenty-three. Indeed, Burroughs had long since claimed that there were no coincidences, but the leaps that his brain was making to piece so-called evidence together were becoming greater and greater. Wherever he saw the number twenty-three, he inferred some negative meaning, and wherever he saw something negative, he looked for the number twenty-three. That was largely how his brain had always worked, and why he had gotten into so many bizarre areas of study and engaged in so many ill-conceived quests, psychic or otherwise.

In August he was writing again for the *International Times*, describing the theories of L. Ron Hubbard. He explains that unconscious people register sounds and that these sounds create engrams. However, given his recent turn away from Scientology, it is unsurprising that he moves on to describe how this information can be used by Scientology auditors to gain control over other people:

> "The film unrolls 1913 style dim perky far away
> we see a man on a couch. He is being audited.
> The auditor sits at the head of the couch. The
> subject on the couch goes through a pantomime
> of fear shame hate impotent rage like a puppet on
> invisible wires as his infantile traumas are run. He

gets up thumps his chest and wrings the auditor's
hand. He is 'clear.' He starts for the door. Not
so fast my old beauty. The auditor pulls back the
curtain to reveal a hidden tape recorder."

The story continues as the auditor offers the man a tape recorder
which will reduce any person to a state of absolute despair and
subservience. The man accepts, and goes around witnessing the
effects. Then another man goes through auditing but declines
to carry the tape recorder with him. He is thrown out on the
street and subject to a vast conspiracy of all persons affected
by the tape recordings. Death and violence ensues, as well as
suppression of personal freedoms, before eventually the tape
from the tape recorder evolves into a giant tapeworm.

This story, never reprinted anywhere else, marks the high-
point of Burroughs' hatred of Scientology at this stage in his life,
and is certainly one of the better pieces of writing on the subject.
It is Burroughs at his absurd, violent, and satirical best. Over
the coming years the majority his writings both in favor of and
against Scientology would be non-fiction, but would lack sort
of punch delivered by his decidedly chaotic short story. Here
Burroughs says more about Scientology in what he calls "word
sludge" than in any of his carefully composed essays.

In 1967, Burroughs' fame was making him valuable property,
and he frequently appeared in men's magazines in addition to the
pantheon of small literary rags that he graced during the sixties.
These provided him with a steady income, and in particular he
enjoyed a fruitful relationship with the pornographic magazine,
Mayfair. Burroughs was friends with the magazine's deputy
editor, Graham Masterton, who suggested the idea of a column,
in which Burroughs would expound upon his bizarre theories.
Burroughs decided that it should be called The Burroughs
Academy, and the concept was that his weird ideas would come
across as lessons. He remained interested in the idea of an actual
bricks-and-mortar academy over the next decade, and some of
his books, like *The Wild Boys* and *Port of Saints*, deal with the
sort of revolution that his ideas were intended to bring about.

In October he was interviewed by *Mayfair* (a painfully staged interview with him and Ginsberg, in which Burroughs comes up with the idea for his column), and also contributed the first column, called "The Future of Sex and Drugs." The series would go on for nearly two years, and would explore many of Burroughs' interests in the area of fringe science – from Scientology to death whistles. He was effectively writing the sort of material that he would have read and believed as a boy. In this first issue, Burroughs tackled the idea of the word in relation to Korzybski's General Semantics, and later he would continue to outline his theories on life, including the Mayans and hieroglyphics, and so forth.

Masterton explained,

> "He was now talking a great deal about Scientology and L. Ron Hubbard and although he was intrigued by the concept of engrams and becoming a 'clear' he was extremely scathing about Hubbard himself and his Sea Org. I suggested to him that he write an article about it for Mayfair…"

In the November issue, Burroughs contributed an essay called "The Engram Theory," highlighting his apparently renewed interest in Scientology. The piece masqueraded as investigative journalism, and the tagline (written by Masterton) claims that Burroughs was exploring the topic of engrams because "To play someone's engrams back to them can cause intense distress. They could control the minds of a whole society," suggesting that Burroughs held some sort of fear that the Church of Scientology might be in some way dangerous. The idea, Burroughs agreed, was Masterton's, even though he had already considered writing his own hack-job of Hubbard. By late August, however, his antipathy appears to have subsided, and although he claims Hubbard's writing is "atrocious," he also acknowledges "the importance of his concepts." It seems that he was already planning a fairly positive article.

To complete this assignment, on September 10th Burroughs' editor drove him and Antony Balch to the Scientology Center, where they used pseudonyms and attempted to sneak around the premises. In Masterton's words:

> "William suggested that he and I go to Saint Hill the British headquarters of Scientology in East Grinstead on what he called 'a reconnaissance mission' with -- yes -- the clear intention of exposing Scientology not so much as charlatanism but as (and I quote) 'a highly effective technology in the hands of assholes.' I rented a car and we drove down there with Antony Balch filming us and taking photographs. Somewhere there must still be a surviving movie of that visit but I have no idea who has it now. We entered Saint Hill under assumed names, William Lee and Graham Thomas, and a toothy lady showed us around. On the way back to London, William said that he had decided that he would probably enroll in Scientology and try to become a 'clear'… He was enthused by the science and the psychology of Scientology although he still had nothing complimentary to say about L. Ron."

They had called ahead of time and requested an interview, but were turned down – neither Hubbard nor anyone else was willing to speak to the press, which is hardly surprising given the headlines of the day. However, the Scientologists were fairly accommodating when they actually showed up, and gladly showed them around – no sneaking required.

Burroughs spent the remainder of the month writing his article, and read every Hubbard text that he could find by way of research. It appears to have had a huge impact upon him, for he attended Academy training at the London Org in September, completing his study materials by the 19th. On his "Student's Basic Checklist" is an impressive array of reading and listening material that Burroughs signed off on in a remarkably short period of time, as from his prior study much of this material would already have been familiar to him.

On October 1st, he wrote to Gysin with details of the trip:

> "The trip to St. Hill was amusing though I thought we would never arrive in one piece... Anyhow we took a lot of movies of St. Hill and scientology at work, they didn't seem to mind at all. Writing the article I bought and carefully studied all of L. Ron Hubbard's published work I could locate. Most interesting. Clearly the rank and file are given a few tricks and the extensions held back. That is by the fact that of practicing the tricks they are given they come under the influence of those who know the extensions of these elementary tricks."

Burroughs goes on to say that he has studied some of Scientology's "tricks" and has created his own "extensions." He speculated that it might be dangerous to publish, but that maybe it would work as part of his collaboration with Gysin, *The Third Mind*. About the article, which by this stage was written but not yet published, he says it is "restrained" and is obviously holding back some criticism and some kudos. He claims that he is "giving Hubbard his due, raising some doubts and reservations."

Reading the essay, it is hard to see how Burroughs could have come to the conclusion that it was "restrained," or how the editor came to produce a tagline that suggested any negative views would be presented by the author. It is severely lacking in criticism, and as such it fails as a piece of investigative journalism. However, the essay presents an intelligent and remarkably well-read breakdown of the basic principles behind Scientology. He also demonstrates an understanding of Hubbard's ideas that was previously absent from his correspondence. Moreover, it is unusual to read Burroughs' coherent prose, as for seven years his work was dominated by cut-ups and even in his letters he shunned grammar. From his 1959 letters to Allen Ginsberg to the short essays he wrote for his own understanding between 1962 and 1964, we were able to see his interest and his understanding grow, but by the end of 1967, the year before Burroughs enrolled in a course at the Church's headquarters, he was able to demonstrate an advanced knowledge that made him a leading authority on Scientology. No doubt this was due to the extensive reading that he outlined to Gysin.

The essay begins:

> "The importance of L. Ron Hubbard's theories as expressed in his book *Dianetics* and a number of subsequent books and bulletins is enormous. It is no exaggeration to say that anyone who wants to understand the destructive techniques used by the CIA and other agencies official and private must read Hubbard's writings and must read them carefully. Very important data is often dropped in quite at random."

He goes on to describe Hubbard's ideas, in particular focusing on engrams, in remarkably clear language. Objectivity is lacking, and at times it seems like Burroughs is simply advertising Scientology, which isn't particularly new or surprising, given that he suggests it as a method of resisting control in several of his novels. He even displays his own bias and lack of scientific credibility when he says, "The evidence in favour of Hubbard's basic assumption [the engram theory] seems to me overwhelming." The evidence in question appears to be Hubbard's books, coupled with some of Burroughs' own opinions. Nothing concrete, of course, or verified by the scientific community.

Burroughs comes close to criticism when he brings up the suggestion – as promised in the essay's tagline – that perhaps engrams could be used as a weapon. If an organization were to record "word combos" and play them to people, he says, it could be used for mind control or even the complete destruction of a person's mind. But Burroughs never even suggests that perhaps the Church of Scientology could do such a thing. Again displaying an amazing bias, Burroughs concludes his short section on the dangers of engram study: "He says that pain drug hypnosis could conquer a country faster than any atom bomb. You can say that again, Mr. Hubbard." Burroughs goes on to suggest that secret organizations around the world want to get their hands on this weapon, but that Scientology is effectively guarding against them.

It is only in the final section of the essay that Burroughs admits doubts about Hubbard, whilst still maintaining his position of overall approval of Scientology and the theory of engrams. He suggests that it may be possible for a preclear to "dump" his engrams on another person, making himself clear whilst harming another. In Burroughs' letter to Gysin he claims that this is "deplorable," if true. However, in his essay he holds back and says,

> "There is much which I think is valid in Mr. Hubbard's writing. I am convinced that his engram theory is substantially correct and that silence in operating rooms and in the vicinity of unconscious persons would prove a prophylactic measure of incalculable importance. However, I do not agree with any exercise in passing along what is wrong with you even in an imaginary context. From imagination to precise practice is a short step."

Burroughs' notion is that engrams can function as a virus, and he references Hubbard's claim that a preclear, under the guidance of a trained auditor, could theoretically pass along his engrams to another person. He attempted to question Hubbard about this idea, but when he visited Saint Hill to research his article, Hubbard was not there. Burroughs' only real criticism throughout the essay is more or less lost in the midst of ecstatic praise for Scientology, suggested exercises, and reading lists, but oddly it ends by extending a sliver of doubt: "We find much that is useful, much that is truly revolutionary and profound, and yet quite a lot with which we cannot agree." It appears from the essay, though, that there really wasn't much of Hubbard's writing with which Burroughs didn't agree. It never seems to occur to him that Scientology could be employing its own methods of control, and he touts it heavily as the key to resistance. He seems absolutely convinced of its inherent good, despite his distrust for other organizations.

A few days after writing to Gysin, but before the article was yet published, Burroughs even went as far as to recommend Scientology to his son, Billy, who was now out of rehab:

> "You should study dianetics and scientology which is certainly the most workable system in existence and to me is much more interesting than any of the Eastern systems. I will send you some books on the subject which I have just been studying to prepare an article. Point about scientology is that it works. In fact it works so well as to be highly dangerous in the wrong hands."

He continues by saying that Hubbard is "uneven as a writer and a thinker," with some great ideas and some fairly tedious ones, "so you have to read every word very carefully." He says that he is sending some basic materials, and if Billy is interested, he will send along some more advanced ones, as well as a copy of his article. He claims "to have found scientology very useful for writing and have in fact devised a system of my own derived from it." At the end, he mentions studying karate and aikido, to which he made frequent brief references in the mid-sixties, and which would pop up during his tenure at *Mayfair*.

Having gone through a short period of antipathy towards Hubbard and his organization, and having gotten to the extent that he wished to use his writing as a weapon against them, it is amazing that by the end of 1967, Burroughs' views have flipped and he is once again an advocate of Scientology. Indeed, he was so impressed with his short course at the London Org that he decided to sign up for a more serious training course, and a follow-up essay, in January of the following year. If Burroughs' essay in the November issue of *Mayfair* read like an advertisement for Scientology, then his follow-up in January reads like a hopeless ode to the religion penned by its most dedicated follower.

Clear:
1968

Saint Hill Manor was purchased by L. Ron Hubbard in 1959 as a training center for Scientologists. The year Burroughs enrolled for his first training course, the brochure fawned over the building's impressive setting and history. It is written with Hubbard's unmistakably trite and self-aggrandizing phrasing, not to mention his fondness for the word "free" and its derivatives:

> "Throughout the history of Man, one reads of Man's continual efforts to free himself from bondage, slavery and ignorance... Scientology has found the answers and the Road to Total Freedom."

He goes on to mention England's clichéd "green fields" and "rolling hills," and even is as audacious as to suggest a warm and sunny climate, thanks to the "Gulf stream [blowing] across the Atlantic from the Caribbean." He talks about the county's "10,000 years" of history with "many major events." However,

> "These events don't compare, in any way, to the current historic events or the contribution being made to mankind at Saint Hill now… The ultimate developments of Scientology by L. Ron Hubbard at Saint Hill is an achievement without equal in the annals of history, and is indeed history in the making."

The brochure is illustrated with photos of young men and women (mostly women) in ridiculous poses, smiling and laughing, reminiscent of boxes from old board games. Again, Hubbard's overblown language comes clearly across in the captions: "laugh gorgeously," "graceful," "serene," and "delightful." Finally, the brochure concludes by claiming: "Saint Hill is a shining beacon for all to reach for in a world that is dark through ignorance and misery."

If this sounds a little over-the-top, it is nothing compared to the essay which Burroughs produced after enrolling at Saint Hill in the Hubbard Trained Scientologist Course. It was printed in the January edition of *Mayfair*, and was titled "Scientology Revisited." The tagline would have surprised anyone who had read his previous essay, which read more or less as an advertisement for the organization:

> "I had a number of misconceptions about Scientology – the lurid expectations of a secret and sinister cult. But, as I learned more, I had a final conviction that Scientology does point out a whole new way of looking at this universe."

At the editor's admission, there were probably few customers who actually took the time to read Burroughs' essays, or indeed any of the text printed in the magazine. *Mayfair* was pornographic and its "readers" largely had one intention when opening it. But anyone who had read "The Engram Theory" would be surprised to know that Burroughs harbored any negative thoughts about Hubbard or his Church. Indeed, it is odd to see Burroughs even use the words "sinister" or "cult," but perhaps that was just a way of grabbing attention. At the time, public opinion regarding Scientology was on a severe downwards slope, and having been thoroughly impressed by his visits, by the literature, and by a brief time spent enrolled in a training course, Burroughs was ready to take on the international media by arguing – without the use of cut-ups – that there was nothing objectionable about Hubbard or Scientology.

The essay opens with yet more silliness. He states that its purpose is to correct errors in "The Engram Theory," and points out that it was intended simply to act as an overview of the religion – with Burroughs suggesting that he had expected to find something awful, but that he had managed to offer a "critical approach to the literature of Scientology." There are less ridiculous phrases attributed to the naked women throughout the magazine. It becomes apparent that the point of this essay is simply to erase any doubts he had left in the minds of his readers that Scientology is the most important system of belief in the world, and that this essay was going to be even less "critical" than the first.

Had he not already lost the respect of his readers, Burroughs quickly moves into heaping praise upon L. Ron Hubbard as a writer, saying that although "he does sound rather like a visitor from outer space who has taken a refresher course in how to address the natives on their own level," his writing is nonetheless "clear and precise" and that he is "more a technician and an organizer than an artist."

Not satisfied with throwing his literary credentials out the window, he moves quickly into his only new complaint: that the name Scientology opens the organization to mockery. He paints the scene at a snooty literary dinner party, where the guests mock the oddness of the name and suggest it is just "another cult" from Southern California, owned and operated by hippies. But once again, Burroughs draws upon his old favorite, Korzybski, who once famously pointed at a chair and claimed it was anything but a chair. "Whatever Scientology may be it is not the label the word 'Scientology.'" In the end, it is the people who mock Scientology, in Burroughs' mind, who are foolish.

Soon he's correcting himself by removing any doubt over the problems and misuses of Hubbard's discoveries:

> "What I said in Bulletin 2 relative to the misuses of Scientology in the wrong hands is all too accurate. The best insurance against the misuse of Scientology is afforded by the open dissemination of information, processing and training offered at 37 Fitzroy Street, London and Saint Hill, East Grinstead, Sussex. There is nothing secret about Scientology, no talk of initiates, secret doctrines or hidden knowledge."

He continues by suggesting that there are secret organizations around the world out to control the human race by stealing Scientology's methods, and that all negative publicity aimed at Hubbard is pure propaganda by these same forces. He says that "facts" don't matter because the media will always lie to cover for the powers that wish to do evil.

The media, whose anti-Scientology reports Burroughs had previously believed to be accurate, remains the focus of his next tirade:

> "An accusation brought against Scientology in the press is of course 'brain washing,' the implication being that anything which alters thinking is bad by nature. It is of course understandable that those individuals who profit from keeping the public in ignorance and degradation do not want their thinking altered in any way and most particularly not in the direction of freedom from past conditioning which they have carefully

installed."

After a few weeks of studying Scientology, Burroughs himself appears somewhat brainwashed, and can't see the irony in his argument.

It is amazing just how enthusiastic he sounds in this essay, not only for the engram theory and the E-meter, but for every aspect of Scientology, including Hubbard. Despite earlier reservations, and later criticism, he appears absolutely won over, and is bent on disavowing his own suggestions that Scientology may be less than perfect, and especially eager to contradict the media's attacks. He even defends Hubbard's reputation by saying, his "degrees and credentials seem hardly relevant. Dianetics and Scientology are his credentials and he needs no others." Of course, by this stage Hubbard's past had already been under intense scrutiny. But such criticisms never stopped Burroughs from defending Reich, and they weren't about to sway him to the dark side in regards his new hero.

Having satisfied himself that he had put to the sword any doubts about the brilliance of Scientology, and having cleared his conscience for having questioned it in his November essay, Burroughs moves on to describe his experiences on the training course. But not before listing the address of the center (again), its opening hours, rules, and even the price of the course (a very reasonable thirty pounds per week).[1] He claims that the course will make you smarter, so that you don't just learn Hubbard's teachings quickly, but you can improve your ability to learn anything. You can also remove annoying mannerisms, and make yourself more socially adept – something that no doubt would have served Burroughs well as an awkward young man. In a telling turn of phrase, he even claims that Scientology could help people who have been socially "handicapped for years."

Burroughs goes on to describe the auditing process, and in particular the use of the E-meter. He describes the process

---

1 Graham Masterton explained: "We never had any adverse reaction to William's initial enthusiasm for Scientology, even when he appeared to be advertising it. Mayfair was totally against censorship of any kind, sexual or political."

in general, before claiming that it is all true – "anyone who undergoes processing" knows that engrams are real and that auditing works. However, Burroughs' claim to objectivity is again shot when he reveals his own experiences, seemingly by accident, whilst trying to stay out of the story:

> "There is a moment when the incident is quite clear and then suddenly fades like old film as the needle floats. There is a sort of click in the head when this happens. You can *feel* the needle float."

By revealing that he underwent auditing and that it seems to have had the same effect he got from drugs or his orgone accumulators, he is giving away probably more than he intended. Again, to him it is proof. Scientology is a matter of *facts*. But to anyone bringing a critical mind to his descriptions, he sounds like another convert to a cult, drugged and brainwashed by false promises.

In his conclusion, Burroughs weighs up the benefits of Scientology against his own life experiences:

> "As one who wasted four years and thousands of dollars on psycho-analysis I can testify that Scientology processing administered by a competent professional can do more in five hours than psycho-analysis can do in five years."

He continues by reminding his readers that Scientology is not just a means to erase bad memories and enhance our abilities, but is also an essential element of the fight against mind control through language, and ends by saying that it shares common ideas with Hassan ibn Sabbah – something that surely would have only served to further alienate any of the magazine's readership.

A less balanced essay there could hardly be, but "Scientology Revisited" is invaluable evidence in uncovering the importance of the religion in Burroughs' life. Most interestingly, it shows just how impressionable the man was. When he first learned about Scientology from Brion Gysin in Paris, Burroughs was aware of some of the negative sides to the religion, and demonstrated in the following years some minor reservations. Yet the more he studied, the fewer reservations he had. He viewed it first and foremost as a means of freeing himself from systems of control – something of benefit for the whole of humanity. By the end of January 1968, after a few short weeks of auditing, he appears as dedicated as the follower of any cult – and his knee-jerk reaction is to dismiss his own previous doubts, along with the protestations of any naysayers outside the organization. This essay marks the high-point of his obsession. For seven years his enthusiasm built to this point, and one doubts any person alive could have successfully remonstrated with him over Scientology's dark side. This is most likely because Scientology was becoming more than just a weapon in the fight against the word virus, but was becoming a tool to heal himself. All his life Burroughs sought such things. He was a deeply scarred human being with a mind full of awful memories and what he perceived as handicaps – his homosexuality and drug addictions. He had sought to fix his problems through therapy, yet evidently Scientology was a quicker and more effective fix. As intelligent as Burroughs was, he was nonetheless fragile, and as wary as he was of being a "mark," he was so desperate to find a cure for his pains that he would have walked into any trap set just for him. And looking back at his history of beliefs, and his long line of particular problems, no trap was as custom-made for this man as the Church of Scientology.

On his first day at Saint Hill, Burroughs sat in the auditing room and the process started. In Scientology, the communication cycle – with which Burroughs was already familiar because of his prior study – is rigid and follows a pattern that is odd to the outside observer. In material that Burroughs later studied and kept, Hubbard explained "To add words to the patter is to risk restimulation and it is expressly forbidden to do so." It is also forbidden for auditors to give any sort of opinion as a response to the preclear: "Above all, don't be critical of the pc." The cycle is carefully designed, and is said to have effects similar to hypnosis. It is intense and can produce hallucinations, and supposedly even out-of-body experiences. In Burroughs' case, the auditor began by posing a series of questions. The preclear in this case is allowed to answer in any way except by leaving his chair, and Burroughs – recounted in an interview with Bill Morgan – appears to have been somewhat provocative in return. When the auditor asked him what he would say if he met the president, Burroughs replied, "Drug hysteria." As part of the cycle, the auditor must coax the preclear to elaborate, and Burroughs went on to say that he would ask the president, "What are you trying to do, turn America into a nation of rats? Our pioneer ancestors would piss in their graves." To the pope, Burroughs claimed he would say, "Sure as shit, they will multiply their assholes into the polluted seas."

The auditor then ended the session for a break, after which they continued by addressing overts and withholds. The purpose of this session is to explore some more obvious traumas and issues with the preclear. In this case, the subject of Kiki – the boy Burroughs had fallen in love with in Tangier – came up. Burroughs explained that Kiki had died, and began to talk about how he felt. In Scientology, however, it is not important to go into depth about such things, and the auditor pushed Burroughs instead to picture Kiki, going back in his memory to the clothes that Kiki wore. When pushed back into his memories, being able to see and hear and smell things as though they were happening again, Burroughs blacked out. When he woke up, the auditor told him that he'd experienced a "Rock C slam" – in other words, a particularly strong reaction had registered on the E-meter.

Incidents such as the above, which are available to the analytic mind, are known as "secondaries" – and are used to guide auditors to engrams. In the beginning they are powerful and can have effects like Burroughs suffered. But replaying the trauma, guiding the preclear from the beginning of the memory to the end, over and over, is said to render the engram powerless. Sometimes neither the auditor nor the preclear can understand what the problem is, or why it is being released, but in Burroughs' case he found it immensely therapeutic. For him the phrases that would give a floating needle were mostly "quotes from my own work or someone else." In one instance he found "hieroglyphics" registered as a floating needle, signaling that an engram has been run. Other release points included the phrase "Why, it's just an old movie," a meeting he could barely remember with a man called Lord Montague, the British museum, the phrase "sharp smell of weeds from old Westerns," and the character of Scobie from Graham Greene's novel, *The Heart of the Matter*. Sometimes his words were like cut-ups: "The emerald beginning and end of word." He didn't necessarily understand exactly what was going on, but Burroughs was sufficiently relieved of pain that only a short while into his course, he wrote the *Mayfair* essay, "Scientology Revisited."

During these secondaries, Burroughs noticed that the word "emerald" kept popping up. Twice it marked a release, but he didn't know why. His auditor told him that this could mean an attachment to a "suppressive person," or maybe a place or object, and he was told to go through a process called "S&D"[2] wherein "you simply list items and then check on the E-meter." Burroughs ran through some obvious possibilities, but then considered that it might be, as the auditor said, "an object." He suggested the word "emerald," and got a floating needle. "That's it," the auditor said. Burroughs never understood the importance of the word.

From the Hubbard Trained Scientologist Course in January, Burroughs quickly moved on to Auditing to Grade IV Release, Power Processing, and the Solo Audit Course. In all, the courses were intensive and lasted up to eight hours a day, five days a week, and went on for several months. The Solo Audit Course alone took two months of intensive study to complete, and required listening to sixty hours of Hubbard speaking on tape. During this time he lived in a shared house with six or seven

---

2 S&D – search and discovery

other Scientologists,[3] returning to his own apartment only on weekends. Sommerville found him intolerable during this period, as Burroughs attempted to audit everyone around him (including the poet, Harold Norse, who Burroughs claimed reacted with enthusiasm), and went on at length about Scientology. He claimed Burroughs would give him his "Operating Thetan glare," which deeply disturbed Sommerville.

In his letters to Gysin, Burroughs is somewhat restrained. Gysin was never a member of the Church of Scientology and merely found it interesting, and in his letters over the intervening decade it seems Burroughs is trying to downplay his own enthusiasm, and sometimes to rekindle Gysin's. Shortly after starting back at Saint Hill in January, he wrote Gysin to say that he had been "reinstated" (as though he'd been thrown out), and then offers a pithy excuse for going back for more:

> "The fact is that processing has uncovered a lot of extremely useable literary material and dreams now have a new dimension of clarity and narrative continuity. I have already made more than the money put out on stories and material directly attributable to processing. So might as well follow through and see what turns up."

Perhaps referring to this argument, Gysin would later joke that Burroughs was just about the only person to have made more money from Scientology than they had taken from him. Later in his letter, Burroughs talks about viruses, and references Hubbard several times, indicating that his own views were being changed quite substantially having resumed his Scientology studies. In another letter he repeats the "reinstated" claim and goes on immediately to talk about the number of men on the course. "The whole organization has been inundated with males and we are now in a majority." He tries to win Gysin over with the number

---

3 In an unpublished essay, he says six, but in his later review of Robert Kaufman's *Inside Scientology*, he uses material from the same essay, but claims that there were seven housemates, and describes the building as a cottage, located five miles away from Saint Hill.

of men around, with claims that the auditing procedure induces a state that brings about naturally spoken cut-ups, and the fact that Balch and Harold Norse had been processed.

At some point during his time at Saint Hill, after finishing up his Power Processing course but prior to being declared clear, Burroughs wrote an essay called "Power." This essay remains unpublished, however, parts were paraphrased and included in a Scientology magazine over the summer. There is nothing in the essay to suggest that Burroughs had anything but positive thoughts about his experience on the course, and we can assume that he at least knew that other Scientologists would read it, but he does daringly suggest improvements upon the system. It begins by outlining the traditional view of power: nations with armies, police forces, and money. But, he says, these thing "come and go and are no more. The power that remains is the power each individual has within himself." He goes on to explain how the most important force in the universe is a clear, and finishes up by giving his personal testimony:

> "This is the power released by power processing. This power is the abilities regained after release from counter forces that have blocked the individual from the use of these abilities. Once regained these powers cannot be taken away from the individual. It is <u>his</u> power. Power processing is release from whole track engrams experienced over thousands of years. That this release can be effected in a few hours demonstrates the point of perfection achieved by Scientology technology. It is not necessary to locate them and run out thousands of such moments any more than we need to excise each individual germ to be cured of an illness. To run each engram would take a life time of auditing. The technology pin points a few whole track engrams and clears these on the E-meter. The P C knows as well as the auditor when the needle floats. Anyone who experiences

power processing knows that he has been released
and that he has regained <u>his</u> power that he can
now apply to his life and his work."

Whilst studying auditing, Burroughs became interested in
the idea of exteriorization – when a person's spirit, soul, or
conscious energy form leaves the body. He produced a cut-up of
some Scientology literature regarding this technique, and mixed
it with some of his thoughts about using tape recorders. "Ask
the preclear to be a foot back of his head," he says, quoting an
early instruction. There is also reference to "pressor beams,"
which are a form of concentrated energy, much like a laser,
that high-level Scientologists are supposedly able to produce.
Burroughs was very interested in lasers at this point, and had
always been interested shifts in time and space, so his interest is
unsurprising.

In another unpublished essay written the following year,
Burroughs recalls his time living at Saint Hill as his enthusiasm
began to wane under the stress and rigid nature of life there. It
begins, "Now to give you an idea of what St. Hill was like in my
day." He describes living with six young Scientologists, including
females who "come on with cognitions and embarrassing thinly
disguised sexual dreams about Ron like young nuns dreaming of
Christ." Together they would all drive at top speed to get to their
classes on time, as punishments were strict. If they were late, they
had to wear a grey rag tied around their arm, signifying that they
were in a condition of Liability. As if this wasn't embarrassing
enough, they were forbidden from eating lunch, as well as from
shaving or washing, during this period of punishment, and to
end it they were required to collect signatures to a petition in
order to absolve them of their sin.

Despite his years of studying, Burroughs recalled being
constantly in fear of failing the E-meter. He compared himself
to young women with "high tone arm" and said that "fear stirs in
my stomach" whenever he thought of the device. He described
his "twin" – the person primarily responsible for auditing him –
as "a nice middle-aged woman from California, I would judge

she's buried three husbands $250,000 a coffin." The supervisors could be particularly harsh, and reduced some of the women to tears. To Burroughs they'd say, "You're in a condition of danger." Telling the story years later, Burroughs liked to present the people around him as military types, barking orders, marching preclears about the building, and making them line up.

Indeed, Burroughs was coming to the attention of the authorities. Although his opinions regarding the genius of Hubbard's ideas were unchanged, his attitude towards being controlled was predictable. He had never been good at obeying rules or doing what he was told, and whilst at Saint Hill he did admirably in fighting his urges to rebel. But he was still subjected to the dreaded Sec Check – a formidable list of questions designed to weed out potentially disruptive students. He claimed that so many students were being dragged into Sec Checks that he was required to perform his in a broom closet with "some grim old biddy." The first question was: "Do you feel that St. Hill is a safe environment?" Burroughs claims to have replied: "It's so safe its overwhelming gee I never felt like this before you know what I mean like belonging to something big," whilst later adding, "All this time I felt my self respect slipping away from me and finally complete gone as it were officially removed."[4] All this was recorded on the E-meter, which is basically a lie detector, and other questions included: "Are you here for any other reason than you say you are?" "Do you have any doubts about Scientology?" and "Do you harbor any unkind thoughts about L. Ron Hubbard?"

This last question posed a problem for Burroughs, who was quickly becoming sickened of the cult of personality around Hubbard, but he supposedly managed to fire off a quick reply that satisfied his interrogators: "Well, I just can't help being jealous of someone who is so perfect." In a remarkably short time he had grown to hate the man's "big fat face," and although he still respected his ideas, he went home to his apartment at the weekend and fired his air gun at photos of Hubbard he stuck

1 This is nearly a quote from Céline • "*All this time I felt my self-respect* slipping away from me and finally completely gone. As it were, officially removed."

on his wall in a crude attempt at a curse. One time the hammer of his gun snapped back and very nearly broke his thumb, and Burroughs felt that that Hubbard had somehow managed to return the curse.

According to the essay, Burroughs viewed himself as an anthropologist attempting to "penetrate a savage tribe… to get the bog medicine he has come for." His initial exposure to the inside of the religion had convinced him that it was pure and good, but having dug a little deeper, he claimed to despise it and was simply searching for a cure to his own problems before escaping.

Still, one should keep in mind that this essay was written around a year later, and at the time Burroughs appeared utterly captivated by the Church of Scientology. His later references to the time at Saint Hill were far more negative than his notes and letters from the time, indicating that he exaggerated or spun his stories later, when his opinions had soured. While at Saint Hill, he wrote to friends, recommending that they, too, get audited, and although he acknowledges that Hubbard is a poor writer, he pushes his theories on the recipients of his correspondence from Saint Hill. On the Solo Audit Course, he wrote Gysin to say, "I am interested to really learn the subject having already profited professionally." He clearly had a sincere drive to learn and advance in the religion.

The Solo Audit Course was the hardest part of Burroughs' time at Saint Hill, taking him around two busy months to complete, but he learned a lot and found it satisfying. He wrote Gysin,

> "I am still on the solo audit course where one learns how to solo audit a procedure now used on all advanced grades… There are sixty hours of tapes to hear. Hubbard can't write but he can talk. You read the bulletins and don't get it, but when he explains it in a taped lecture you do *understand* it. The actual auditing necessary to clear this level is about two to five hours. The technology is now so precise that little auditing

126

time is necessary. About forty hours to become clear. There are now eight grades above clear where you learn to leave the body at will and be at cause over your environs. We shall see. I plan to take the clearing course and one of the levels above that then see how the abilities gained can be applied to writing."

It is interesting to note that he often referenced a perceived improvement upon a writer's abilities stemming from auditing, which was a major motivation for him during difficult points on the course. He goes on to talk about people on the course – there were about seventy students - who reminded him of faces from his past, including Bill Belli, Paul and Jane Bowles, Gregory Corso (who Burroughs jokes is an operating thetan), and his wives, Ilse and Joan.

In May Burroughs was asked to take the Joberg – a list of 104 questions "about every criminal activity you could conceive of" – which was of course carried out at his own expense. He claimed that it was because he "rockslammed" a question during a Sec Check – "What would have to happen before Scientology worked on everybody?" The Joberg list of questions included some weird, depraved crimes against laws and morality, including having sex with your own mother, as well as taking drugs, running a baby farm, or hiding a corpse. This was all recorded on the E-meter and to pass required a flat reading for every single question. When asked, "Have you ever concealed a body?" Burroughs' answer gave a positive read, and he explained, "I think it's Whole Track," referring to past lives. He had a vision of himself in ancient Egypt, and when the question was rephrased to extend only to "this life," Burroughs said "no" and there was a flat reading. When they asked him if he'd ever forged anything, he said "no" again, having legitimately forgotten about his days forging prescriptions. The E-meter had actually remembered something that he had forgotten, and even in his hatred of the process, he was impressed.

During break time, other Scientologists would try to get

the truth from him outside the test room, and Burroughs was disgusted by the attitude of these people, willing to turn stool pigeon in order to advance. They would ask him things like, "What do you think of Ron's new directives?" and he'd reply, "Oh, I'm sure Ron knows what he's doing," and laugh. Later he would descend into routines that had Hubbard being turned in by over-zealous followers and subjected to the test. He even joked that the vending machine could be placed in a condition of "Non-Existence for refusing to work."[5]

During this period, Burroughs had easy access to Scientology's Auditor's Report Forms and used them to note down some of his cut-ups. There are a series of cut-ups on these forms that all take from the same unspecified material. The first of these is titled "Cut up with John Cooke's Tarot Card Book." In 1967, John Cooke had published *The New Tarot Card for the Aquarian Age*, which Burroughs had read. In another untitled page of cut-ups, Burroughs has text that contains similar words, phrases, and themes. Even though it appears that the majority of the material used was from different sources, it seems that he was cutting some of his own writing – the same pieces of writing, time and again – into the cut-ups. Throughout these pieces we have repetition of the words "pale," "ghost," "spit blood," "St. Louis," "thin pale boy," "weapon," "under," "handcuff," etc. There are naval and Biblical themes scattered throughout. Different dates are scattered through the pieces – "April 3rd, 1882," "April, 1923," "910 B.C." and different names: "John Cooke" (not used in the piece with his name in the title), "Dave Moor," "Jim Who," and even a reference to himself. There is a sense of the dark and also the erotic throughout the cut-ups, and the image of childhood is ever-present.

On May 30th, the Church of Scientology opened a new center in Edinburgh, called Advanced Org, and Burroughs signed up for its Clearing Course. Prior to that he had been planning on taking the course in Valencia, and then popping over to Tangier for a visit once clear. Despite having cleared the Joberg, he was required to take yet another Sec Check before progressing

5 Non-Existence – Scientologists belief you can "unmock" things to stop them from existing.

further, and this time he was asked about possible affiliations with the Communist Party, and eventually he admitted that he had attempted a curse against Hubbard. Amazingly, he passed and was admitted onto his final course. It was the first time Burroughs had retuned since the Festival conference in 1962, but he loved Edinburgh and was glad to be back. He was one of the first students enrolled on the course, and tested clear on June 15th, after eighty hours of auditing. "Quite spectacular results," he wrote Gysin. He was declared Clear #1163, and had passed through the various levels of Scientology in remarkable time. In their magazine, *Advance*, his achievement was celebrated by the Church of Scientology, and Burroughs was touted as an "Internationally famous American writer." The article quotes him as saying, "It feels marvelous! Things you've had all your life, things you think nothing can be done about – suddenly they're not there anymore!" It goes even further:

> "Throughout his training and processing, Burroughs has made immense gains in his ability as a top professional writer, to start and finish major literary work. The day after his Power Processing, he wrote, effortlessly, a chapter he had been struggling with for the previous month. Just prior to commencing the Clearing Course at the Advanced Org, he wrote an excellent film script, his first, in a remarkably short time."[6]

Burroughs is later quoted as saying, "Whatever anyone does, he will do it better after processing." It claims that Burroughs is working on a new novel, in which Scientology features as a "primary factor in the destiny of Mankind," and that he is now enrolled in an Operating Thetan course, and "moving forward strongly on the road to Total Power." Operating Thetan is an even

---

6 Compare this with his essay, "Power": "The day after my release I sat down and wrote with no effort a chapter I had been trying for the past month. Even the typing was easier... I can testify that my ability to create fictional characters and situations has quite measurably increased with Scientology."

higher state of being than clear, according to Scientologists.

Despite this claim, and other claims that he would continue to study beyond the Clearing Course, Burroughs instead dropped out of the Church and returned to life in London with Sommerville. "Scientology was useful to me until it became a religion," he later explained. Still, though he was left a little disillusioned by what he now considered to be a cult, his enthusiasm for Scientology's methods and ideas had certainly not abated. Burroughs was on an auditing bender, putting up posters around London and auditing anyone who'd sit long enough. Sommerville quickly grew weary of Burroughs' behavior and moved out of their Duke Street flat. According to Morgan's biography, Burroughs was close friends with John McMaster during this period, whom Morgan noted was an ex-Scientologist.[7] In fact, McMaster's defection from the Church didn't occur until November, 1969. At this point McMaster was still contributing to Scientology's *Advance* magazine, and acting as Hubbard's personal spokesman. He reportedly told Burroughs that he was Rudolph Valentino in a past life, something that he had also mentioned to the press on several occasions, but Burroughs was decidedly unimpressed. Still, they remained friends for many years.

He was also fervently working on a project involving materials taken from Saint Hill. He was cutting up Clearing Course materials and, he wrote Gysin, getting "remarkable results." Although his descriptions of the project are vague, he seemed to be transcribing lectures and auditing tapes. "The experiments to date have showed how to cut up. Now we know *what* to cut up." Since his earliest visits to Scientology centers, Burroughs seems to have viewed their materials as possessing some sort of quality that made them desirable for his literary reinterpretations. He also writes that "the reactive mind is the biologic weapon of

---

7 Testament to the lack of importance both Miles and Morgan give Scientology in their biographies, and Grauerholz gives in his commentary for *Word Virus*, they all incorrectly named McMaster "McMasters." Grauerholz claims that Graham McMasterton introduced the two men, but Masterton denies this, having never met McMaster.

female invaders." This might just have been another attempt to convince the misogynistic Gysin of Hubbard's genius, but Burroughs was entering the worst phase of his own misogyny, and such comments are hardly unusual for this period.

Given Burroughs' experiences over his months at Saint Hill one might have expected something more from his *Mayfair* column – either another enthusiastic parading of Scientology as humanity's savior, or perhaps a more fair and balanced approach, as he was now well acquainted with its lesser points. However, during his time on the course the column focused on other topics, including pictorial language (both Egyptian and Mayan), karate, and visions of societal oppression in the not-so-distant future. In the June issue, he was more interested in describing flicker and ruminating on experiments with tape recorders and cameras, and in July he offers an overview of the Burroughs Academy. In the latter he lists the lessons his students should have taken from his columns to-date, with Burroughs playing the role of teacher. First there is Scientology, but it is not given the fanfare it earlier received, and indeed Burroughs gives scant few details about why it is so important. He suggests that his students "stop doing everything you 'have to do'" and begin instead visualizing these things, and run them repeatedly until they realize how unimportant these things are, thereby robbing them of their power. This is, of course, a technique taught in Scientology. Burroughs moves on to list the other important elements in the Burroughs Academy – karate, aikido, yoga, Egyptian hieroglyphics, black magic, virology, linguistics, General Semantics, and talks at length about Reich and his Deadly Orgone Radiation theories. He ends by suggesting that his course has the ability to greatly improve the human situation, and uses Hubbard to explain:

> "What is a problem? Mr. Hubbard has defined a problem as postulate counter postulate, inattention counter inattention. The brain artifact has a built in mechanism that prevents it from solving problems and that mechanism is The Word. The Brain can only produce more survival

131

artifacts that produce more problems. In this last course we have rubbed out the word."

On July 16th, Burroughs wrote one of his best essays in favor of Scientology, linking his training with his perceived improvements as a writer, called "New Dimensions in Writing."[8] Sadly, like many of Burroughs' thoughts on Scientology from 1968, this essay would also go unpublished. It details precisely the connection he saw between Scientology's method of processing and its perceived impact upon his writing. In 1959 he had been convinced that Scientology would be of benefit to him as a writer and had told Allen Ginsberg that everything he wrote ought to be subjected to the methods of Scientology, and evidently during his time at Saint Hill, almost ten years later, he had become even more certain of this fact. As this essay demonstrates, even with his contempt for Hubbard and other elements within the Church, he was still convinced that his abilities as a writer were benefiting from Scientology.

> "In 1959 Brion Gysin wrote: 'Writing is fifty years behind painting.' Why this gap? Because the painter can touch and handle his medium and the writer cannot... I think that Scientology can close this gap and give a whole new dimension to writing. Scientology can show the writer what words are and put him in tactile communication with his medium. Scientology is the first precise science of words and how certain word combinations produce certain effects on the human nervous system."[9]

He goes on to state that in higher level auditing, one learns to be

8 This essay appears to have been written for the benefit of the Church of Scientology – possibly for them to use as promotional material. Burroughs sent the essay to a member of the organization, along with a letter claiming that it would be followed by another essay detailing the benefits of Scientology for the average student.
9 This passage was salvaged and reused in *The Job*.

careful with words because of their potential dangers. From the general subject of writing and Scientology, he goes on to a more personal approach:

> "In the lower grades of processing I achieved discipline and better working habits. I learned to complete cycles of actions and not leave half done projects behind me that decrease the ability to concentrate. After Level VI and Clear I was able for the first time to handle my specific disabilities as a writer. I realized that my writing had become over experimental and that I was out of communication with my readers. Now experiments are valuable and a writer should experiment with words. However there is a danger that the writer will become so involved in experimental techniques that he loses contact with his audience."

Burroughs explains that he had wanted for some time to write a straightforward novel with a beginning, middle, and end, but that he simply didn't believe he could do it. He was compulsively drawn to experiments "that were becoming increasingly sterile." He claims to have written and sold a screenplay that more than covered all the money he'd paid for Scientology training, but that it was worthwhile: "Now that the clearing course has freed me from disabilities I find that I can write whatever I choose to write... Processing has paid for itself even financially."

He continues:

> "Now consider the widespread idea that writers write because they are aberrated and would lose their talent if they were cured of aberration. Edmund Bergler, a well known psycho-analyst, flatly states that there are no normal writers. What does doctor Bergler mean by normal? He means exactly the type of individual Mr Hubbard

uses as a model of aberration… The Scientology definition of the non-aberrated person is the precise opposite of the psychiatric definition: The non-aberrated Scientologist is one who has regained his abilities. The psychiatric definition may well involve a loss of abilities."

Burroughs concludes:

"The first gain of clearing for a writer is the ability to appraise his own work to see where he fails and why and to correct his failures. From a few months of processing I have learned more about my profession than I could have learned in twenty years without processing. I have learned that I can make things go right in writing, that I can eliminate errors and failures. I am convinced that when more writers take the clearing course completely new and unexplored horizons will be open to the writer freed for the first time from crippling disabilities."

Here again is a reference to "disabilities." In the January edition *Mayfair* he had written about Scientology's ability to cure a man's "handicap." Burroughs had always viewed himself as deeply flawed, scarred by awful events in his past, and it seems that he is connecting his developments as a writer to Scientology's removal of these problems.

However, if he still appeared to be dishing out unrestrained praise for Scientology in public, or to members of the Church, Burroughs was more honest in private. To Graham Masterton he seemed angered by his experiences:

"I saw much less of him when he actually enrolled for the course but when he had finished it and talked about his experience I had the feeling that he was infuriated that such interesting technology should be used by Scientologists to impose what he considered to be an oppressive and almost fascistic regime... Mind you, he was aggrieved about a lot of things, especially the way that big business in his opinion had deliberately suppressed such boons as everlasting lightbulbs and socks that never wore out and the Tucker car."[10]

A month later, in August, Burroughs travelled to the United States to attend the Democratic Convention in Chicago as part of a reporting team for *Esquire* – another men's magazine. Alongside Terry Southern and Jean Genet, Burroughs patrolled the streets of Chicago with his tape recorder, recording the sounds of rioting and playing it back in an attempt to change reality, to break apart the messages fed into the thousands of soft machines in the streets. He called these his "reactive mind tapes," and claimed they were "fantastically successful in stirring up trouble." Hunter S. Thompson was there, so was Normal Mailer, and Allen Ginsberg, who was handing out acid and attempting to bring about peace instead of the violence that was looming. It was a violent year in America, with the assassinations of Robert Kennedy and Martin Luther King, anti-war demonstrations, police brutality, and riots in more than one hundred cities. Burroughs was shocked but also impressed by the determination of a generation of youth he and his Beat friends had helped inspire, and lamented that in the UK such rebellion was impossible. He then traveled to New York, where he wrote the article and saw Jack Kerouac for the last time. He was horrified at Kerouac's appearance. His old friend had deteriorated terribly thanks to his rampant alcoholism.

In his *Esquire* article, Burroughs connected his street recordings to the reactive mind:

"Deconditioning   means   the   removal   of

10 In 1948, Preston Tucker designed an innovative but controversial new car, whose development was stopped thanks to interference by the established automotive industry. For years Burroughs remained interested in the Tucker car as a symbol of the suppression of new ideas.

all automatic reactions deriving from past conditioning... all automatic reactions to Queen, Country, Pope, President, Generalissmo, Allah, Christ, Fidel Castro, The Communist Party, the CIA... When automatic reactions are no longer operative you are in a position to make up your mind."

He later elaborated:

"It's more of a cultural takeover, a way of altering the consciousness of people rather than a way of directly obtaining political control... As soon as you start recording situations and playing them back on the street you are creating a new reality. When you play back a street recording, people think they're hearing real street sounds and they're not. You're tampering with their actual reality."

In his August column for *Mayfair*, he also ties Scientology to audio and visual recordings, but in a very different way. He explains, without explicitly referencing Scientology or Hubbard, an important idea from *Dianetics*: that the human brain stores every piece of information that it encounters, although this information is not necessarily available to the conscious or analytic mind. "You can use your mind as a camera," he says, and looks back over moments from his own life – "that day you'd forgotten, those friends you no longer know." He uses the word "recall" as a noun, which was often used by Hubbard. Burroughs also suggests that it is possible to see into the future, to view "memories" of things that have not yet happened. Throughout the article he also makes reference to "present time."

The September issue again references film and Scientology. Burroughs has two characters act out the difficulties of life, and one of them begins to explore the idea of escaping from "present time." This phrase, from Scientology, is repeated again and again. He explains, "Present Time is a film and if you are *on set* in present time you don't feel present time because you are in it." The idea of just walking off set is raised, although Burroughs refrains from his usual explicit instructions and does not openly suggest a method for leaving the film set.

Writing to Antony Balch from his New York hotel room in September, Burroughs talked again about Scientology in relation to his tape recordings from Chicago. We can clearly see that he is repeating ideas from *The Soft Machine*, where his character brought down the Mayan priests' mind control system with cut-up recordings of everyday sounds:

> "Just in passing the reactive mind tapes are fantastically successful when it comes to stirring up a spot of trouble. And I have talked to scientologists here who went clear in half an hour… And maybe all the dangers of the clearing material is simply resulting from the fact that they have all your auditing reports and can turn on the buttons if you don't want to go clear their way."

The danger Burroughs appears to be referring to is the notion that once you have run your engrams with an auditor, you have let yourself become vulnerable. As Burroughs demonstrated to himself, tapes loaded with stimuli can be used to devastating effect, and it would be possible for Scientologists to create a tape specifically for a person, likely a suppressive, to trigger their engrams, causing pain and suffering or, perhaps, preprogrammed actions. Here Burroughs is switching from the view that Scientology is a means to resist control to finally realizing that it is itself a form of control, perhaps equating it with the Mayan priests. Indeed, he is alluding to what his reader may have expected from his "The Engram Theory" essay in *Mayfair* – a step in logic that he was at that time unable to make.

Burroughs was also interested in the idea that course materials read or heard out of context could make people sick, which was a claim made by Hubbard. With John Giorno, Burroughs had made cut-up tapes with Clearing Course materials and "I Am That I Am," and experienced no negative effects. They even played these tapes at a poetry reading in Central Park.

> "Clearing course only makes some one sick *if he has been processed or trained in scientology*. In short each grade of processing is implanted in previous grade, you got it? That is why all this insistence on the same words and no contact with defectors. So what you get from the clearing course done my way is immunity from the attacks of scientologists."

His October column marks a slight shift in attitude, and in the tagline Scientology is referred to again as "a cult." The editor goes to length to explain that this is a piece of fiction based upon reality, and in particular a visit Burroughs paid to Saint Hill a year earlier, when doing research for *Mayfair*. He says that the interview contained within the text is a "reconstruction" of one that Burroughs actually conducted. The editor who wrote the tagline was Graham Masterton, who drove Burroughs to Saint Hill on that first visit. It's unlikely that any of the story is true, as it sounds straight out of Burroughs' imagination, with Saint Hill merely used as a back drop at one point. Like *Naked Lunch*, the setting changes seamlessly from one continent to another, in this case from South America to the Saint Hill Manor to a concentration camp. There are monsters, and characters seem to dissolve into the backdrop. Burroughs is seeking answers about a virus. The only real connection to Scientology, aside from the location, is that he used the same name for one of his characters as the fake name under which he first explored Saint Hill, and a reference to "exteriorization" – an advanced part of Scientology training in which Burroughs had once been interested. When discussing exteriorization, he says, "Years ago I had studied something called scientology I believe." The story was later published in the 1973 collection, *Exterminator!*

Burroughs returned to London in October, and took up with a

young hustler he had met through Balch, called John Culverwell, now that Sommerville had effectively parted from Burroughs' life. Culverwell supposedly had "love" and "hate" tattooed on his knuckles, which would've played into Burroughs interest in Scientology, because the processing method utilizes opposing phrases. He was surprisingly happy to be back in London, but that probably stemmed from the peace and quiet he had there, which allowed him time and space to write. That month, Daniel Odier interviewed Burroughs extensively for a book that was released in France in 1969 as *Entretiens avec William Burroughs*, and then in English in 1970 as *The Job*. This book has been the subject of a great amount of quote-mining, as it catches Burroughs at his most extreme and paranoid. His misogyny is on display more than at any other point in his career ("women are a biological mistake"), and he talks readily about many of his interests and obsessions from over the years. He describes himself in a letter to Gysin as "messianic" in the book, and says that "people are ready to listen." When Odier asked him a question Burroughs would talk at length. The English language version of the book contained essays and other material by Burroughs, some collected after the release of the French version, in addition to the interviews, and throughout it he expounds on his ideas about Scientology.

Leaving aside the essays that were written and added later, there is plenty of evidence of his opinions about Scientology during 1968, some as answers to Odier's questions, and others lifted from his *Mayfair* column or elsewhere. He tirades against the prevailing interest in money that has resulted in the suppression of important innovations, medical and otherwise, citing as evidence Scientology, orgone accumulators, and large doses of vitamins E and A. He goes on to describe the process of "mocking up" as taught in Scientology and several times describes the importance of silence, especially during childbirth and space travel. He also describes again his proposed academy, which really just sounds like a Scientology training center.

Before talking with Odier about *The Job*, Burroughs had planned on producing a book called *Academy 23*, which is referred to frequently throughout his correspondence. This would have included material from his *Mayfair* articles, coupled with parts of *The Wild Boys*. Instead, Burroughs managed to get across most of his wild theories and revolutionary tactics in *The Job*, and *The Wild Boys* came together satisfactorily as a novel. "Academy 23: A Deconditioning" was published in an anthology called *Notes from the New Underground* in late 1968. Parts of what was meant to be *Academy 23* spilled over into the *Revised Boy Scout Manual*, which was later released as a cassette. In *Revised Boy Scout Manual* Burroughs gives explicit details on how he believes a guerrilla war should be conducted, eventually running through an example of how it could overrun the United Kingdom, culminating in chants of "Bugger the Queen!" Vital weapons included in this scenario are orgone accumulators, the Cut-up Method, and killer whistles. He also listed the creation of a calendar as the most important aspect following a revolution. In 1970, Burroughs would adopt his own calendar for a year.

His increasing weirdness was on display in another series of interviews, conducted with Jeff Shero of *The Rat*, also published in *San Francisco Express Times*. Following his experiences in Chicago, Burroughs became increasingly politicized, claiming that he was finished with writing and more interested in getting out into the street to "make trouble for everybody!" Indeed, throughout the middle and late stages of the decade, he makes more frequent references to the youth of the world, and a cynic might say the old man was just trying to stay relevant to the people most likely to buy his books. He appears to be positioning himself as a part of the revolution. His books had been full of tools to fight the forces of control, but now he was on the front lines, having carried his tape recorder into Chicago, and addressing the forces via the medium of the underground press. "Well, I'm all for eliminating the whole stupid bourgeois middle class," he said. "I think the whole strata should be eliminated... They're not alive. They're talking tape recorders." Soon he is talking about technology and government suppression of ideas, including Reich and Hubbard, as well as a laser that can push people under a truck.[11]

In late October he wrote Gysin with reference to his collaboration with Balch, mentioning that they are "rolling around with the reactive mind film in spare time." He displays an unusually hostile attitude towards Hubbard, suggesting an awareness that Hubbard was using Scientology to make money. He claims to have discovered Hubbard "has 7 million dollars in Swiss bank account," and says of Scientology, "I don't want anything more to do with these scruffy people." Around this time, newspapers were reporting – correctly – that Hubbard had been engaged in numerous shady business practices, and was indeed making a lot of money from Scientology, despite claiming to earn less than the Church's paid staff. In another letter he says that he wanted to see the movie, *2001: A Space Odyssey*, largely because it was forbidden for Scientologists to see it.[12]

He extends his criticisms in a letter to Joe Gross, stating "The technology is interesting but I am in flat disagreement with their policy." Tellingly, he asks why they even need a policy, as Burroughs had always been opposed to such rigid systems. He complains about "subservience to the dictums of L. Ron Hubbard," and a total lack of interest in research. He does, however, shower praise upon the E-meter. "It is amazingly accurate in gauging mental reactions," he says, and again ponders its relationship with encephalography.

This attitude is unusual, for in the January issue of *Mayfair*, presumably written in November or December, Burroughs is still showing respect for Hubbard, comparing him to Reich and others as men of genius whose work is covered up by evil organizations.

"The medical profession is suppressing Reich's orgone accumulator and his discoveries relative

---

11 The incident in question was something Burroughs read about in *Ramparts* (although he erroneously places it as *Esquire* in his interview) and refers to it in *The Job* and a *Mayfair* article from 1969. His growing paranoia saw him becoming afraid of laundry vans as a method of CIA surveillance.
12 A bulletin from the time explains that the movie "produces heavy and unnecessary restimulation."

to the use and dangers of orgonic energy. They are suppressing Dianetics and Scientology discovered by Mr. L. Ron Hubbard... As you know Reich's books and papers were burned, his experiments outlawed and he himself imprisoned... Mr. L. Ron Hubbard, the founder of Dianetics and Scientology, has also been persecuted by the Pure Food and Drug Department. To date Mr. Hubbard has refused to publish his advanced discoveries. There is every indication that the discoveries of Scientology are being used by the CIA and other official agencies. With these discoveries already in the worst possible hands it is to be hoped that Mr. Hubbard will reverse his present policies. To Mr. Hubbard belongs the credit for making public a secret weapon used extensively by the Americans and the Russians in their dreary cold-war farce."[13]

Burroughs goes on to suggest that Reich and Hubbard's discoveries have been covered-up or discredited by government agencies because they touch upon sensitive information. He states again that the CIA and other forces are using techniques that Scientology could well combat, and it is therefore in the best interests of those agencies to suppress Hubbard's ideas. It sounds like Burroughs is largely repeating his ideas from a year earlier, when he wrote "The Engram Theory" for *Mayfair*.

It is clear from looking at his life and works that Burroughs connected and developed his obsessions, which became part of his own unique worldview. Everything was connected for him, and in one obsession he would look for evidence of another – for example, he justified cut-ups with Scientology and Scientology with cut-ups. Throughout the mid-sixties he was absolutely obsessed with the apomorphine cure and sent numerous letters and wrote countless articles in order to spread its influence. By late 1968 he had come to the conclusion that "the reactive mind

13 This passage was also included alongside his interview with *The Rat* and reprinted in *The Job* as an answer to an interview question.

mirrors the regulatory mechanism of the body." Therefore, if apomorphine stimulates the hypothalamus in order to regulate the body's metabolism, that would mean the reactive mind has a physical location within the brain – the hypothalamus. He speculates that the people who control the world are aware of the location of the reactive mind, and that's why they are so bent on suppressing apomorphine. Once again, Burroughs is justifying his obsessions – apomorphine proves the existence of reactive mind, and the reactive mind explains why apomorphine is not accepted by the medical community at large.

In December Burroughs still had his eye on Hubbard, particularly in the newspapers. Over the coming years he would carefully read these tabloid stories, but believed almost everything that was said. He wrote Gysin that,

> "Mr Hubbard... has abolished security checks
> and is even trying to give his pamphlets a more
> literate air. The government here refuses to divulge
> the reasons for the Hubbard exclusion act and
> the ban on visiting scientologists... Hummmm,
> sounds like they have turned up CIA connections.
> Meanwhile Hubbard is wooing Greece on the
> isle of Corfu and has rechristened *The Royal
> Scotsman* — purchased in Nigeria and flying the
> Panamanian flag — *The Apollo*."

In addition to his work for Mayfair, Burroughs was busy putting together *The Wild Boys*, and working on a film script about Dutch Schultz, a mobster whose final words were taken down by a police stenographer as a string of stream-of-consciousness gibberish that Burroughs thought was a sort of natural cut-up. He had been working on *The Wild Boys* since early 1967, with a large part of it written afterhours during his time at Saint Hill. Both projects, Burroughs explained, were given structure by his understanding of the reactive mind.

Suppressive:
1969-1997

Chief among Burroughs' complaints about Scientology was the way it treated its outsiders, and on January 27th, 1969, he was to become one of them. An HCO Ethics Order[1] on that date said:

> "WILLIAM BURROUGHS of 8 Duke St., St. James Rd, London SW1 is hereby declared in a condition of Treason.
>
> "Burroughs by his own admission has written out from memory 'Clearing Course' material and Pr. Pr. Commands and has run some 300 hrs. of 'Squirrel Techniques' on himself (for 'experimental' purposes).
>
> "By his own statement Burroughs is of the opinion the Confidential materials should be freely publicised and that there would be a largely

---

1 HCO – Hubbard Communication Office

scope for these materials in Universities.

"And with these actions Burroughs has betrayed the trust bestowed in him with Confidential materials.

"And with these actions he has taken himself off the road to Total Freedom. He is not to enter any Scientology Church of Organisation. His is not to be trained or processed and may never again be admitted to Advanced Courses. ,

"The formula for treason is 'FIND OUT <u>THAT</u> YOU ARE.' He is to follow the formula."

Jargon and odd phrasing aside, this note may seem bizarre to those unfamiliar with the Church of Scientology, but Burroughs would have been more than aware of their attitude to the people known as "suppressives." In fact, much of the criticism lobbied at the Church during the sixties related to their treatment of former Scientologists.

Although he was familiar with their treatment of suppressives, and although he had already turned his back on the Church, with the official condition of treason came a change in attitude. Burroughs had certainly gotten sick of certain elements of Scientology during his time studying the religion, but he continued with enthusiasm in the months after being declared clear. He hadn't spoken out publically against Hubbard or the Church, and one might even speculate that his coolness towards the religion was just a momentary blip brought on by the stress of the intensive course.

However, with his expulsion from the religion came out and out war. Burroughs probably hadn't expected it. He had continued to study and practice as a squirrel, and in doing so he was in his mind still carrying out Hubbard's ideas. He knew the rules, but he was hardly doing anything worthy of the description, "treason." Still, what he did he did publically. Burroughs was, as the Scientology magazines described him, "internationally famous." Eyes were on him. The Church was aware of his affiliation with *Mayfair*, and were delighted that for once a journalist had investigated the religion and produced a positive report, instead of joining the ranks in denouncing it as a cult. Although he wasn't about to give up what he perceived to be its valuable lessons, Burroughs fired back a response to Bill Flemming, the man who'd signed his condition of treason notice:

> "While I continue to call attention to the importance of Mr. Hubbard's discoveries and endeavor to obtain for these discoveries the serious consideration they merit, I find myself in disagreement with many points of policy... I feel that the assumption of having studying Scientology I am thereby committed to acceptance of all Scientology policy is unwarranted. I am not an organization man."

He went on to stress that the Church of Scientology should have no control over what he, as a writer, should be allowed to publish, and concluded by stating that he and the Church would simply have to "agree to disagree."

In March Burroughs was as obsessed as ever about the E-meter, regardless of his position in regards Hubbard or the Church. Probably more enthusiastic about it than most Scientologists, he believed it was a device of immeasurable importance, capable of solving any problem. It wasn't just engrams that it would make disappear. Even people and abstract problems could vanish if you really wanted them to. He wrote Gysin:

> "Have been giving most of my time to the E-meter for the past two weeks following discovery that *anything* or *anybody* can be as-ised[2] and made to disappear by running flat on E-meter. This takes some doing and items run out in intricate webs of association relating to similar incidents

---

2 As-is – another term of Scientologese. A verb meaning to see something as it is. The opposite is "not-is", meaning to deny or reject something. "It is immediately apparent that all governments run on the not-is principle," he says in the column.

and persons. No need for the O.T. courses which are strictly Indian giving leaving the organization in a position to take back what they gave. All the courses and processes leave unflattened incidents behind that can be restimulated at any time... I am sure you could run your financial problems with excellent results and will send you along the instruction books explaining use of the E-meter if you are interested. The money process consists in one command 'Mock up a way to waste money,' repeated until the needle floats. Point is when a problem or person floats on the E-meter there is an immediate change in the external situation. For example John [Culverwell] left... (he nearly got married in fact). I had just gotten a floating needle on sexual blocks and personnel involved therein when the phone rang and John was calling to ask if the job was still open."

When Sommerville called and complained that there was a burst water pipe outside his flat, causing a noisy traffic jam, Burroughs told him to run the sound on an E-meter, and the next day traffic was diverted. "Flattening an item is often followed by immediate alteration of external situation," Burroughs explained. He even speculated that if African-Americans armed themselves with E-meters, they could end racism across the U.S. He sent instruction pamphlets to Gysin, along with his own detailed and hopelessly optimistic guide to using the E-meter.

During April and May, Burroughs was in correspondence with John Cooke, the man who'd first taught Gysin about Scientology. They traded opinions about some fundamental aspects of Scientology, such as what it means to be a clear, and also bitched about Hubbard. Cooke compared him to a confused child. However, he maintained a certain fondness for his old friend. Referring to the incident in Algiers, he said of Hubbard, "I hope I am there to help him over the hump, even tho he failed me when I needed him," and then added, "I am not bitter... I

147

love him." Now that Burroughs had been cleared and then put in a Condition of Treason, he was able to see the Church from a similar perspective, and to state his views more precisely and logically than before. He explains that Scientology was very helpful for him, but that as a religion or organization, he no longer had much use for it:

> "It seems that Mr Hubbard is playing an all out power game and cannot allow anyone capable of insight and intelligent evaluation of data in the organization. It's very much like the purge of the Old Bolsheviks. What it all amounts to is a monopoly of magic to be dispensed on their terms. Total freedom indeed. However the Clearing Course was worth all the Sec Checks and nonsense. A vital key to the computerized methods of thought control actually in use by official agencies and one can't help wondering if there isn't a degree of *cooperation* involved. I find the E-meter very useful for pinpointing psychic areas and eliminating interference."

In May Burroughs was interviewed by the underground newspaper, *International Times*, on the subject of deconditioning. After discussing his Cut-up Method, Burroughs got to talking about Scientology.

> "The E-meter seems to me a useful device for deconditioning. I have reservations about some of the Scientology technology, and grave reservations about their policy as an organisation. I feel there's an absolute incompatibility between organisational policy and the advancement of knowledge, as we see in the Communist party where people are forbidden to write certain things or even to discover certain things, because it doesn't fit with a preconceived policy. I feel

that Scientologists are tending to get into that
impasse of having a dogmatic policy."

He elaborates further:

> "They have a great deal of very precise data on
> words and the effects produced by words – a real
> science of communication. But I feel that their
> presentation has been often deplorable and that
> as a science, a body of knowledge, it is definitely
> being vitiated by a dogmatic policy."

After stating these drawbacks, Burroughs' attitude towards
Scientology improves as he focuses on their methods. They
discuss therapy and resolutions to mental and physical health
problems, and Burroughs' enthusiasm for the E-meter is evident.
It crops up throughout the interview in relation to various other
theories, and Burroughs is always confident in its abilities. Still,
he is adamant that the technology must be used in association with
other fields and experts from other areas in order to maximize
its potential. He suggests that people should purchase their own
E-meter (listing the price as a very reasonable £42) and run
themselves at home, rather than engaging with the Church of
Scientology.

That same month, Burroughs' *Mayfair* column also focused
on the subject of the E-meter. Throughout it, he delights in
explaining in depth just how this piece of equipment works.
You would never know this was written by a man who has been
excommunicated by the religion, as he sounds as devoted as ever
– again giving the price of an E-meter, and even recommending
that his readers sign up for a training course (clearly contradicting
his advice from the *International Times* interview). He does a
good job of breaking down the functions and purposes of the
device, getting into fairly complicated territory but putting forth
the information in a concise manner. He also brings up an idea
of Hubbard's that he hadn't before publically discussed that
all humans have in them opposing goals; one positive and one

negative. For example, in every person there is the goal to win and the goal to lose, the drive to make a good impression, and an equal drive to make a negative impression. The E-meter can be used to "as-is" the less desirable goal, which is part of the reactive mind and therefore impossible to otherwise influence. The idea of these opposing goals intrigued Burroughs and was used in writing *The Wild Boys*.

In 1969 Burroughs wrote seven short pieces that were sent out to various publications, all under the heading "Abstract." These abstracts share similar styles and also closely resemble parts of *The Wild Boys*, which is hardly unusual as Burroughs frequently used submissions to small publications as practice for writing his books. They are often visual pieces, laid out like film scripts, highlighting Burroughs' interest in film at the time, and also feature cut-ups. Sometimes they are narrative, sometimes purely instructional, and sometimes both mixed together. We commonly see a juxtaposition of images, positive and negative, in a reference to Hubbard's idea. The first two abstracts were published by *Lip*, and the first of these focused on the Scientology auditing procedure. It presents and then runs negative images like engrams in a demonstration of how these can be robbed of their damaging power, resulting in a state of pure happiness. Near the beginning, in a line of questions and answers presented as per processing, there is a discussion of the nature of the reactive mind. Burroughs ties it to Egyptian hieroglyphics and the Mayans, and states that it is 12,000 years old. "What is the origin of the Reactive Mind?" he asked. "Abstract," he answers, suggesting that the very function of these pieces, and arguably *The Wild Boys* novel, was a demonstration or exploration of the functions of the reactive mind. The second abstract does not directly refer to Hubbard or Scientology, but employs the same tactic of presenting negative images for the purpose of running them. These two pieces were printed in the same issue of *Lip*, in fall, 1969. Another of these abstracts was published in *Klacto/23*, and gave instructions for controlling people via "waking suggestion" – apparently a technique developed by Dr. Dent, who invented the apomorphine cure, although it sounds more like something Burroughs picked up during his time at Saint Hill. Burroughs explains the technique in greater detail in another abstract, published in *Fruit Cup*, where he brings in the use of tape recorders.

By August, Burroughs had more or less finished *The Wild Boys*, although it wasn't published until 1971. It was a move away from the manic cut-ups of the early sixties, with Burroughs later saying, "there was too much rather undifferentiated cut-up material [in the Nova Trilogy], which I eliminated in *The Wild Boys*." Instead, the novel shows Burroughs' interest in film through its oddly styled narrative, and his political leanings are evident in the plot. The "Penny Arcade Peep Show" sections, which came from the above mentioned abstracts, are the most obvious examples, with repetition of numbers and opposing ideas. Burroughs explained that this framework came from "clearing course material." Throughout the book Burroughs is attempting to create mental pictures with his words, rather than to denote meaning, and the use of cut-aways and other film-inspired tricks are helpful. Later he would explain that his incorporation of film techniques in his writing was due to Scientology auditing:

> "...film glimpses will occur in auditing. I don't say you are remembering another life but you are remembering something. A writer always gets his pound of flesh and a number of scenes later used in *The Wild Boys* were remembered on the E-meter."

His visual language aims to bring relative silence to the reader's head, rather than a clutter of phrases. Although Burroughs is no longer advocating Scientology as a weapon, it has become such a part of his worldview that it has influenced his writing style. Incidentally, by August Burroughs had grown bored of his E-meter, saying "I have gone as far as the E-meter can take me and laying off for the present."

In the latter half of 1969 Burroughs was taken by a book called *The Teachings of Don Juan*, by Carlos Castañeda. The book was written by an anthropology student, and concerned the life and ideas of a Navajo shaman. Although it was hit at the time, later its veracity was called into question. In it, the shaman supposedly had drugs that sound loosely similar to yagé, and which cause the user to leave his body. One of Burroughs' chief interests in Scientology was exteriorization, and he applied that term, which is not actually used in the book, in his descriptions of the processes demonstrated. In a 1978 interview, he also cited Don Juan's advocacy of silence as of particular importance.

On October 5th, the *Sunday Times* ran an article about Hubbard's links to the "Wickedest Man in the World," Aleister Crowley. It is typical of media coverage at the time – seeking any connection between Hubbard and anything unwholesome. The article concludes that Hubbard should list Crowley as as much an influence on Scientology as anyone else. Burroughs was interested enough to cut out and keep the story, which featured a large picture of Jack Parsons, rocket scientist and occultist who, like Burroughs saw a strong connection between science and magic. Burroughs cut out the photo of Parsons and wrote "A dream come true," on the back of it.

On October 22nd, Burroughs learned that Kerouac had died two days earlier of a cirrhotic liver – the alcoholic's death. Although they had not been close for a long time, the news hit Burroughs hard, and he slid into a depression that took a long time to shake. Neal Cassady had died the previous year, while Burroughs was at Saint Hill, and it seemed like so many of his friends from the old days were now gone.

In late 1969 the poet Charles Upton wrote and asked Burroughs about Scientology. This helped him realize that his work was responsible for introducing young people to what he could now see was a cult, and he decided to go public with his problems. Burroughs and his friend, the Scottish writer Alexander Trocchi, planned an "underground tabloid" called *M.O.B* (*My Own Business*) with backing from the publisher of *International Times*.[3] The magazine would feature a column called "On

3 Later, in *The Western Lands*, Burroughs suggested that this was also intended to be a TV show.

Call." The intention was to put out a series of magazines with each issue featuring a column dedicated to attacking a "key personality." "Point is to make it as offensive as possible without being legally defamatory," Burroughs explained. People would be put "on call" by being forced to answer absurd questions. "If [the subject] has nothing to hide he will be delighted to answer a few down to earth questions and set his record straight." For the first issue, which was never published, Burroughs wrote an essay attacking L. Ron Hubbard. Although his most famous attack on the religion would come later, it is this unpublished essay that sees him at his vitriolic, sarcastic, and ridiculous best. Although he uses some cut-ups and descends into farcical routines at points, Burroughs is clear and cogent when he wants, and uses logic to devastating effect, demonstrating a tremendous leap from his previous works about Scientology.

He poses rhetorical questions that obviously Hubbard never was never asked, such as, "Did you notice that the head of the Hippie Clan who committed the Tate murders was a former Scientologist?" Of course, Burroughs was referring to Charles Manson, who was notorious as the head of the Manson "family," responsible for the murder of Sharon Tate in August, 1969. Manson had learned about Scientology in prison and was very interested in it, but he never officially joined the organization. His affiliation with the religion was played up in the press, and the mere mention of it was intended as an insult to Scientology. He also asks, "How do you feel about the Church?" "How do you feel about Patriotism and Nations?" "What does Mr. Hubbard feel about the worldwide expansion of police power?" and also asks about the CIA and Vietnam. All of these questions were simply intended to highlight what Burroughs felt was an over-reaching mechanism of control within Scientology, as well as Hubbard's own prejudices.

Aside from these questions, designed to force uncomfortable statements from Hubbard, much of the strength of the essay comes from Burroughs' citations. As a man very well versed in Scientology literature, he was more than prepared for a serious debate, and he quoted liberally from Hubbard's own words.

Rather than take a serious stand, though, Burroughs matches Hubbard with comedy, implying that one couldn't possibly take these statements with any seriousness. He quotes Hubbard as saying, "death camps are being set up in Alaska manned by free thinking, immoral psychiatrists." Despite his own distaste for psychiatry, Burroughs responded:

> "We think that if such camps are being set up in Alaska or anywhere else they are being set up to accommodate 'Hippies, Anarchists, Militants and guideline writers' to quote George Wallace."[4]

Burroughs continued his mockery of Hubbard's anti-psychiatrist remarks by comparing him to an anti-Semite. When Hubbard posited a "secret plan for world domination" by psychiatrists, Burroughs said "the plot for world conquest [is] attributed to International Jewery and The Protocols of Zion." Then he asked whether psychiatrists are communists or not, and claimed that if more people took Hubbard's writing seriously, there would be a "rise of vicious outbreaks of Anti-Semitism."

One of Hubbard's most famous quotes was: "Scientology is a game where everybody wins." Burroughs answered this in his essay by saying, "No losers no game," and asking, "Who is the ANTI-RON?" He adds another of Hubbard's claims: that Scientology offers a "world without crime, without war, without poverty, without illness, without insanity," but as Burroughs points out, this only comes after Hubbard is put in charge as "absolute controller."

Next he attacked Scientology's treatment of outsiders, which was something he had been deeply disturbed by during his time at Saint Hill. Burroughs had long been opposed to the system of ranking applied to humans by Hubbard in his 1951 book, *Science of Survival: Prediction of Human Behavior*. In it, he suggested,

---

4 Racist governor of Alabama who opposed desegregation and claimed that the only people interested in social reform were "left-wing theoreticians, briefcase-totin' bureaucrats, ivory-tower guideline writers, bearded anarchists, smart-aleck editorial writers and pointy-headed professors." Burroughs makes frequent references to him in his letters from 1969.

"The sudden and abrupt deletion of all individuals occupying the lower bands of the tone scale from the social order would result in an almost instant rise in the cultural tone and would interrupt the dwindling spiral into which any society may have entered. It is not necessary to produce a world of clears in order to have a reasonable and worthwhile social order; it is only necessary to delete those individuals who range from 2.0 down, either by processing them enough to get their tone level above the 2.0 line or simply quarantining them from the society."

Burroughs' reply to this is simply: "Just who do you propose to delete around here?" There is not much more one needs to argue in order to make Hubbard's words look evil and foolish. Burroughs also quotes Hubbard as saying "any person from 2 down on the tone scale should not in any thinking society have any civil rights of any kind" and that disposing of them should be done "without sorrow."

The ranking of humans in Scientology is done by way of a "tone scale." This scale gives Hubbard's detailed views on human behavior, and ranks humans from forty ("serenity of beingness") to negative forty ("total failure"). Burroughs, unsurprisingly, was offended that homosexuals were derided as useless for humanity, listed as 1.1 on the scale ("covert hostility") and therefore candidates for Hubbard's proposed deletion. Again Burroughs quotes Hubbard's own words to make him look bad: "In DIANETICS you state that the homosexual is 'so far from normal and so extremely dangerous to society that the tolerance of perversion is as thoroughly bad for society as the punishment of it.'"

Beyond the "deletion" of the uninitiated, Burroughs despised the very idea that those outside the religion were inferior. He disdained the use of the word "wog" to describe non-Scientologists. Although uncommon in American English, wog is a racially disparaging term in the United Kingdom and elsewhere, and Hubbard would have been aware of this fact. It was used commonly among Scientologists, and Hubbard even used it in lectures and some internal communications. To this Burroughs said,

> "You use the word WOG to denote those unversed in Scientology... 'an ordinary humanoid'... as you know the term WOG is used by militant racialists to designate Negroes and Orientals... Isn't this the same as calling them NIGGERS?"

Another issue to which Burroughs had alluded in the past was that of secrecy within the organization. He had claimed in "Scientology Revisited" that there were no secrets held by anyone in Scientology and that it was all put out into the world for the benefit of society. Now he is claiming that the CIA is performing shady experiments and that Scientology is effectively aiding them by keeping their information hidden from the population, who could otherwise use it to fight control. He claimed elsewhere that Hubbard was holding onto secrets, but sometimes that this was a positive thing and sometimes negative. But finally Burroughs attacks Hubbard for this system of money-making and hierarchy, as "confidential materials" are made available only to "upper grades of Scientology processing" and can "only be seen by those who have... paid the fees as laid down by Hubbard." He goes on: "You complain that your discoveries are not being recognized. How can they be recognized by scientists who are not allowed to examine them?"

Although this is a very logical point, it should also be kept in mind that for Burroughs, scientific verification varied in importance. When he believed in something, that was surely enough, and outside approval was not required. He complained about Reich's orgone accumulator not being examined although it was, and he had also alluded to the bias and unreliability of the scientific community. When something he believed in was under attack, it was a conspiracy. He had also explicitly pointed to the limitations of science, such as he perceived them. He mocks Hubbard for claiming to know that his science is sound, yet this had always been his own system of proof.

Burroughs continues to press the matter by asking whether or not Hubbard and Scientology would be willing to open up to the world and have their ideas verified for the good of society: "If Scientology would emerge from a self-imposed isolation and cooperate with workers in other fields... it would have something of value to contribute."

He even went as far as to criticize his beloved E-meter and the fundamental principles behind processing:

> "As we understand it Mr. Hubbard your remedy is to flatten out the E-meter word combinations that produce certain damaging effects until the effects are nullified and erased by repetition? If we had the precise encephalographic coordinates we could simply blank out the intruding patterns... Would you be willing to take part in search that could render present Scientology Tech obsolete?"

He does concede that the E-meter is "very precise" but that it is squandered by a lack of exposure to the general population.

Evidently finished with the logical portion of his attack, Burroughs becomes more abstract and uses routine-like scenes and cut-ups from pamphlets. He begins to sound more like the William S. Burroughs with whom readers are familiar. He mocks Hubbard's pro-American, anti-Communist, and anti-Chinese outlook:

> "The Chinese delegate shits in his pants and screams with rage on TV. The Soviet delegate masturbates uncontrollably. Delegates of all nations rise as one man with tears streaming down radiant faces bellow out THE STAR-SPANGLED BANNER."[5]

---

5 Part of this was taken from *Revised Boy Scout Manual*.

Hubbard's language – Scientologese – is mocked through hilarious made up jargon. Hubbard was known for adding the suffix "-ness" to words, and Burroughs starts listing words that sound like they could've come from a Scientology pamphlet: "IDIOTDISABILITYNESS," "UNWARRENTABLENESS," "INFERIORABILITYNESSES."

This essay is Burroughs at his absolute best, using his more obscure literary weapons sparingly and for the purpose of mockery, whilst setting his mind to the task of destroying Hubbard's credibility. It is this sort of brilliance that makes Burroughs' involvement with Scientology so hard for people to believe. If he was capable of pulling apart the lunacy around the religion, of finding the flaws in Hubbard's language, and the fundamental gaps in logic in his doctrines, then why was he so enamored for so long? For almost a decade he was taken in by Scientology, and although he had doubts from time to time, they seemed to disappear the more he read. What people forget, though, is that Burroughs was a perfect target for people like the Scientologists. He was broken and hurt, confused and seeking something to fix himself. In Scientology he found hope. No matter how brilliant his mind, he was blinded to its flaws because of need. He never fully gave up on some of the ideas, but once Burroughs began to see Scientology for what it was, it all started to fall apart. He was no longer blinded, and he realized it was just another system of control.

Sadly, this brilliant piece of writing went unpublished, along with *M.O.B.* Burroughs did, however, manage to produce one copy. He created a mock newspaper with the headline, "Which side are you on Ron?" alongside a picture of a naked man.

At the end of 1969, Burroughs decided to opt out of the Western calendar and created his own one – the Dream Calendar – which he lived on for one year. The calendar began on December 23rd, 1969 (known as "The Creation") and consisted of ten months of twenty-three days each. The months were named: Terre Haute, Marie Celeste, Bellevue, Seal Point, Harbor Beach, Niño Perdido, Sweet Meadows, and Land's End. On Marie Celeste

5th, 1969, which would have been December 29th in the more conventional style, Burroughs wrote a record of a dream he had experienced.

> "Mr. Hubbard is sitting on a bench. I tell him
> 'You can't date yourself. Time is the presence of
> another being.'
> "I am in a bus loaded with Scientologists inside
> and out. The bus backs into a steep ravine and out
> of control and on the point of overturning. I say
> 'Mr. Hubbard has made a mistake.'"

Four days later, on what was January 2nd to most people, Burroughs wrote something that began like an essay but descended quickly into a bizarre routine. He describes how a person could be coerced into an unconscious state, and then implanted with engrams – visual and audio images that could be easily manipulated "by push button control" by "the Holy Trinity ABC Blessed Arc of the Three Engrams." He demonstrates his knowledge of Scientology by describing precisely how Scientologists could utilize their technology against humans, suggesting that computers and LSD could be used. When confronted by a "playback" of these implanted engrams, the subject will "go mad the way a SUPPRESSIVE PERSON will when he looks at himself... the whole reactive mind is spit at him in ten minutes."

From essay Burroughs switches suddenly to fiction:

> "here smart young liberal college professor gets
> up to advocate the legalization of Marijuana...
> Narc press a button... His hands tremble he sweats
> suddenly he cowers on the platform whimpering
> like a whipped dog."

There are scenes in operating rooms, with doctors and nurses manipulating helpless youths, loading them with negative engrams for the purpose of later torturing them. It is grossly over the top, with nightmarish scenes of control. Next we are taken to a dream sequence. It is set on a train, very similar to the bus in that it's loaded with Scientologists. A man is masturbating when he suddenly gets stabbed in the eye. He is holding a picture of L. Ron Hubbard and shouts, "THANK YOU RON."

In his fiction, particularly the Nova Trilogy, Scientology had always been viewed as a potential weapon or form of defense against such terrifying images of control. This short piece of writing demonstrates that in Burroughs' literary arsenal, Scientology had finally switched sides, and was a tool of the enemy.

Burroughs brought in the New Year by launching his best known attack on the Church of Scientology. It began as article in *The Rat: Subterranean News*, called "Uncle Bill Burroughs (Alias Technically Tilly) on Scientology."[6] The cover proclaimed: "William S. Burroughs (famed author of *The Naked Lunch*) spills the beans on Scientology!" Later in the month it appeared in *Mayfair*, with the brilliant title, "I, William S. Burroughs, Challenge You, L. Ron Hubbard." On the opposing page from the title was a picture of Burroughs staring vacantly into the camera. In March the article was reprinted in the *Los Angeles Free Press* with the less provocative title, "Burroughs on Scientology." This essay was released with the short story, "Ali's Story" in 1978, as "Naked Scientology: An expose of this weird cult," and is widely available online. It begins:

> "In view of the fact that my articles and statements on Scientology may have influenced young people to associate themselves with the so called Church of Scientology, I feel an obligation to make my present views on the subject quite clear."

The essay from there outlines his views of Scientology, although it lacks the clarity, wit, and unique literary value of its unpublished predecessor. Before launching into criticism,

---

6 Bizarrely, "Technical Tilly" is a name usually applied to Ian Sommerville, and not Burroughs. Sommerville is called Technically Tilly in both *The Soft Machine* and *Nova Express*.

Burroughs makes a few concessions: "Some of the techniques are highly valuable and warrant further study and experimentation. The E Meter is a useful device..." From there his first attack is the Church's "organizational policy," which refuses outsiders access to vital technologies. "Suppose Newton had founded a Church of Newtonian Physics and refused to show his formula to anyone who doubted the tenets of Newtonian Physics?" He repeats the point from his unpublished essay that it is wrong to keep these secrets within Scientology.

Next he attacks "Mr. Hubbard's overtly fascist utterances," accusing him of being anti-Chinese, and acting as though Scientology is a guard against the creeping evil of Communism, and mocking his dislike for psychiatry. "Now what is all this flap about psychiatrists? At worst psychiatrists are the defenders of the establishment 'adjusting' or coercing 'deviants' back into socially accepted norms." Just like the previous essay, he references George Wallace, accuses Hubbard of anti-Semitism, mocks the security and secrecy of the Church, and derides its treatment of outsiders.

The latter half of the essay reiterates Burroughs' faith in some of Hubbard's more fundamental concepts – the reactive mind and the engrams – but chastises him for refusing to build upon this with the help of outsiders. Burroughs explains his own theory – that while Hubbard was right in some regards, he was looking in the wrong place for answers. He should not focus on running engrams, but on focusing on other parts of the brain that produce happiness, and "tune conflict out."

Although regrettably an inferior piece of work to the unpublished essay Burroughs had written the previous year, "I, William S. Burroughs, Challenge you, L. Ron Hubbard," was an effective and relatively simple overview of his beliefs at the time, and served its purpose in bringing the Church further into the public glare. It may have lacked the wit, comical vulgarity, and intelligence of the other essay, but it certainly set forth his ideas about Scientology in a logical and reasonable manner. It also brought him to the attention of the Scientology community, and even the man he'd wanted to interview, L. Ron Hubbard.

Immediately after publication of the article in *The Rat*, Burroughs wrote to one of the editors, Gary Thiher, to ask for some copies to send to "disgruntled former Scientologists." He also wanted to know if there were any comments from official Scientology sources. Clearly Burroughs was looking for conflict. In his letter he suggests that Scientology technology was being used by the CIA, and that Hubbard had spilled secrets to the government.

That same day, he wrote to Charles Upton and used the word "fascist" twice to describe Hubbard, and talks about Scientologists as "the most brain-washed followers ever seen." He claims to have read an article in the *Times* wherein Hubbard admitted to working for U.S. Naval intelligence, and speculates then that Scientology is backed by the CIA. His paranoia about the CIA had grown significantly during the late sixties, and he often mentions the agency in relation to Scientology. He goes on to say,

> "I think that scientology is an officially sponsored experiment to test and develop techniques of thought control. And when you see liberal scientologists say, 'Thank You Ron Thank You Ron Thank You Ron,' while he builds concentration camps around them you will realize just how successful the operation is."

Following the publication of his essay in *The Rat*, Burroughs was visited by "a smooth young Jew named Gaiman," who had been sent by the Church of Scientology. This was David Gaiman,[7] who was at that time Deputy Guardian for Public Relations and also Minister of Public Affairs for Scientology Worldwide – a very high ranking member of the Church. Burroughs said that the Church was being conciliatory and seemed positive about Gaiman's visit. He described his visitor as "rather like a friendly well-educated pot-smoking narcotics agent... and very adept at creating the impression that a question has been answered without actually answering it." Burroughs gave Gaiman a copy

7 Father of the author, Neil Gaiman.

of his article (although one would assume Gaiman already had a copy, as discussing it was the purpose of his visit) and said that he would pass it along to Hubbard, although it would take some time.

On January 25th, Burroughs wrote what may have been intended as an essay, column, or letter, but remained unpublished. The arguments contained within were fairly convoluted, with confusing rants, and it was littered with typos. Still, it is fairly typical of his views of Scientology during this period, and the difficulty he sometimes had in attacking what was rather an easy target. It appears that since the publication of his anti-Scientology essay, he was unprepared to deal with a logical, protracted debate. Mostly he just repeated himself, and failed to advance his cause. Whatever it was he attempted to write, he begins by acknowledging that it was, in part, inspired by some feedback regarding his essay in *The Rat*:

> "I have been told by St. Hill that Mr. Hubbard is not to be held responsible for the statements made in FREEDOM SCIENTOLOGY... However Mr. Hubbard must assume responsibility for statements made in the books what he wrotted down."

He continues by comparing Scientology to the Catholic Church (which he had done in his unpublished "On Call" essay, and elsewhere), and makes reference to the CIA again. He reiterates his appeal for Hubbard to join forces with other organizations, and it is clear that some of his ideas are still held as important by Burroughs. He then tells the story of a man who "writes his own orders" from dreams, before cutting them up and following them as instructions. Naturally for the Burroughsian universe, the man runs into people who are expecting him.

In March, Burroughs participated in a discussion for *Playboy*, debating the subject of drugs with a number of well-known or knowledgeable persons. It was here that he coined one of his most famous utterances: "anything that can be accomplished by chemical means can be accomplished by other means." His proof for this statement was that he had studied Scientology, which he describes as a "means of altering consciousness." He goes on to say that "some of the students [at Saint Hill] were former users of cannabis and LSD and they assured me they had never accomplished as much with either of those drugs." He ends the discussion by calling for the creation of academies, which, he claimed, would cure addiction once and for all. His overall sentiment towards Scientology appears unusually positive.

In an interview that month, Burroughs again appears strangely enthusiastic about Hubbard and Scientology. Discussing linguistics, he claims that Korzybski believed Western languages contain "falsifications... that impose aberrative thinking." Korzybski never once used the term "aberrative thinking," and certainly not in *Science and Sanity*, the book to which Burroughs was referring. "Aberrative" is very definitely a term Burroughs picked up from Hubbard, to whom he soon makes another subtle reference. After discussing Korzybski's views on the word "is," Burroughs adds, "A follower of Korzybski has proposed to delete the verb *to be* from the English language." Later, the interviewer asks him whether or not Scientology has proven useful in his work, and Burroughs replies:

> "Some useful techniques and a clear statement of
> very important question: Can man exist without a
> physical body? Can he detach himself from body
> without physical death?"

From 1970 onwards, this idea, stemming from exteriorization, was to be one of Burroughs' prime interests in Scientology, and, as with the reactive mind, he would study it in the light of other viewpoints, developing it and making it his own.

At the end of the month, in the *Los Angeles Free Press*, another of Scientology's Deputy Guardians for Public Relations, Gorden Mustain, offered a reply to Burroughs' essay, called "Organization Electrodes." Breaking down Burroughs' criticisms, he begins by pointing out that one of the publications from which Burroughs took quotes that he attributed to Hubbard was in fact just a Scientology magazine, and it was not written by Hubbard, and therefore "to take the political opinions expressed in this publication and assign them to Mr. Hubbard and then criticize Mr. Hubbard for holding such opinions is an excellent example of the axiomatic definition of stupidity." Mustain goes on to attack Burroughs' views on psychiatry, and denies that Scientology follows any strict organizational structure: "Semantically examined, it is simply a group of individual people working together with agreed upon methods working towards the agreed upon end." He finishes using Burroughs' own words again to say that Scientology's technology is sound: "It works." His defense of the Church, among the first aimed as a response to Burroughs' criticism, was one of the finest. Side-by-side, it is Mustain who comes off best from the first round of debate. Using simple logic, he broke down Burroughs' essay to a few points and answered them clearly but firmly.

Burroughs was getting mail forwarded from the various publications that ran versions of his Scientology article. To one letter, from a Mr. Harr, he wrote back with unusual vitriol aimed at Hubbard, accusing him of "spiritual theft." He goes on to make other accusations:

> "Not only does he not acknowledge but he curses and poisons the sources. Did you know that he stole the E-meter from someone named Floyd Matson, who was then thrown out of the organization and never so far as I know accused Hubbard publicly? So then he turns around and proffers his stolen E-meter as a humble gift to mankind. Shameless son of bitch. Even his curses are stolen from the Crowley sect which he then denounced in his capacity as a member of Naval Intelligence, so he says, or more likely in the capacity of a part time fink."

Still, it is obvious that he at least respects Hubbard enough to view him as a powerful foe, and still gives credence to his ideas, claiming that Scientologists are trained to remove only parts of engrams, leaving just enough left for Hubbard to somehow restimulate them. "As soon as I got into disagreement with him all my so called gains mysteriously disappeared," he claimed, implying that prior to being put into a Condition of Treason, he had all the ascribed attributes of a clear. At this point, he clearly still believes a great deal of what he learned in his Scientology training.

In June, still with no response from L. Ron Hubbard, *Mayfair* printed a reply from his wife, Mary Sue Hubbard, titled, "Mr. Burroughs, You're Wrong About My Husband." In it she defends Scientology quite well against Burroughs' assaults, and certainly with no lack of passion. Like Mustain, she argues the Church's position against psychiatry, states that Scientology has repeatedly tried to work with other groups, but is consistently rebuked, and claims a conspiracy against Scientology perpetrated by the media. She even addresses Burroughs' accusations of racism:

> "You speak of niggers – well at the moment we are the niggers of the press. If a student of Scientology is arrested for drunkness, the headlines scream, 'Scientologist Arrested' and Scientology is blamed for his behaviour. It doesn't matter whether that student had a long history of arrests for drunknesses; the moment he became a student of Scientology, everything changed. This is basically the reason for Scientology ethics. Man, we feel for the black man because we have felt and experienced the same as he."

In August, 1970, Hubbard himself took the time to pen a reply to Burroughs on the pages of *Mayfair*. Like Burroughs, he was careful to offer up one or two kind words before launching into his mild rebuttal: "Burroughs is a great thinker, a searching critic of things in his field. I have no faintest wish to attack him. The world needs their William Burroughses." His rebuttal, though, was more a general denial of all media attacks upon Scientology. He comes across as kind and forgiving – certainly more than Mustain or his wife - and is clearly attempting to put over an image of himself as the benevolent and wise man that Scientologists think of him. Finally, he ends by calling Burroughs his friend, as a friend isn't afraid to offer criticism. Although his arguments were vague and unconvincing, he manages to paint a good picture of himself to help deflect some of the criticisms lobbied at his organization.

Mayfair allowed Burroughs the chance to read Hubbard's rebuttal and to add his own reply for the August issue. Sadly, this only constituted a short passage, wherein Burroughs agrees with Hubbard over the negative influence of mass media (who had been targeting Scientology) and also the ineffectiveness of psychiatry. He is no longer mocking or debating. Burroughs sounds as though he has been reeled back in, and is nearly begging for forgiveness. He makes no new points, nor does he defend any of his earlier arguments. He effectively has admitted defeat, which is sad and strange given the weaknesses in Hubbard's essay. Perhaps Burroughs didn't want to protract the debate, or maybe he had already gotten what he wanted.

While Burroughs' response to Hubbard was disappointingly weak, he took the pages of the *East Village Other* to write his strongly-worded "Open Letter to Mister Gorden Mustain." Burroughs displays clarity and reason well, and demonstrates an ability to take Mustain point-for-point. He begins by saying that it didn't matter if Hubbard never wrote the material in an official Scientology pamphlet as he would have been well aware of it, and any protest would have resulted in an end to it. "Is it… an axiom of stupidity to attribute to Mr. Hubbard at least tacit approval of what was being said in FREEDOM SCIENTOLOGY?" He goes on to address the psychiatry angle: "Every Scientologist who answers my article goes on and on about psychiatry as if the article were an impassioned defense of this dubious profession. I have said frequently that nine out of every ten psychiatrists should be broken down to veterinarians." He goes on to explain that psychiatrists do not control the establishment, but are merely its tools. He rants against corporate power, displaying a surprising liberal bent (throughout the sixties he did appear fairly left-leaning whenever dragged into political matters), and suggests that Scientology is tied in with the powers that be. He attacks the use of the word "freedom" by Scientologists, and says that only the "Liberal Left" truly wants freedom for all people. He then asks,

> "We would like to know where Scientology and Mr. Hubbard stand on the Vietnam war, on sexual freedom, militant students, Black Power, pot, Red China, the policies of the American Narcotics department and the CIA.
> "If it comes to a revolution: which side would you fight on?"

By this stage his argument is somewhat lost. Burroughs is no longer fighting against Scientology, as he concedes entirely that the technology is valid and that their auditing process works. He even concedes the point on psychiatrists, and is arguing semantics when criticizing Mustain for calling him out on quoting a magazine instead of Hubbard. It is only when referring to controversial statements in Hubbard's own books that he appears to make a legitimate counter-offensive, but it is only a short passage in the letter. It seems that Burroughs is now largely clutching at straws, unable to articulate exactly *why* Scientology is so evil. In his letter he is only able to suggest that Scientologists might sympathize with the powers of authority. His language seems intended to stir up young people who are reading the publication, appealing to their reactionary nature rather than attempting to win them over by way of logic. Gone are the wit and perceptive jibes. The Scientologists have put Burroughs on the stand, and he is shaking with nerves.

Burroughs clearly succeeded in provoking a war with the Scientologists, drawing out their highest-ranking members and even the founder and head of their religion, L. Ron Hubbard. Amidst a world-wide attack upon Scientology, Burroughs made his voice heard loud enough to stir them into action (and, for once, not legal action). However, it was a war that he did not win. From this round of fighting, Burroughs came off second best, with the Scientologists ultimately looking to have the upper hand. At the end of the month Burroughs seemed to be running out of criticisms. In a telling example, he wrote to John Cooke, saying "Hubbard has only the vaguest notion as to who Hassan ibn Sabbah was." His insults are scattered and silly, comprised of wild speculation, and hashed together with dubious claims from newspaper reports. His brilliant mind was failing to hit the easiest of targets.

In 1970, on both sides of the Atlantic, *The Job* was released. Originally a collection of interviews with Daniel Odier, published in French, Burroughs had added his own writing, offering essays and extended thoughts to pad out the interview material. Scientology is referenced frequently throughout the book, and notably in essays called "Control" and "The Electronic Revolution," although the latter was only included in later editions of the book, and in 1970 was published in an essay collection of the same name, in German.

Throughout the book, it is clear that there are some points from Scientology that Burroughs accepts unquestioningly. These are no longer theories for him, and in spite of his problems with the Church, these things have become a part of his worldview. In "Control," Burroughs attempts to explain how the Mayan priests controlled their population through the use of their famed calendar. His theory builds upon Hubbard's reactive mind, which for Burroughs is as demonstrably real as anything could be. In the essay, as elsewhere, Burroughs' reactive mind may differ a little from Hubbard's, as he constantly incorporated other ideas into his version. He even speculates where exactly in the brain the reactive mind resides – the hypothalamus. His theory of Mayan mind control requires the reactive mind. Burroughs explains that the reactive mind is an ancient survival mechanism that pre-dates modern language and as such refers to a symbol system.

This was used by priests to make predictions, he says, and is being presently used by other authority figures. But, despite all of his issues with the Church, Scientology is a potential key to freedom from control:

> "Techniques exist to erase the Reactive Mind and achieve a complete freedom from past conditioning and immunity against such conditioning in the future. Scientology processing accomplishes this... The method works. I can testify to that through my own experience."

Hubbard's reactive mind had greatly impacted Burroughs' thoughts on language, and he was constantly looking into ways to "erase" it, or, more accurately, to tune it out. He believed that it may be possible to develop a language that would render the user immune to the reactive mind, taking the tonal Chinese language as an example.

He describes the E-meter, goes into some minor detail about auditing, and mentions that it is a little expensive (which is unusual, because he usually praised the fees as relatively cheap). He also speculates that research into symbol systems may uncover a more effective way to understand the reactive mind. By the second to last paragraph of the essay, one would be forgiven for thinking that Burroughs still possessed a somewhat positive view of Scientology. So far Hubbard is portrayed as the brilliant scientist whose major discovery is the key to curing all the world's ills. However, the final paragraph is lifted from "I, William S. Burroughs, Challenge You, L. Ron Hubbard," and despite sounding grossly out of place, reminds the reader that Burroughs was no more than a squirrel:

> "Mr. Hubbard's overtly fascist utterances (China is the real threat to world peace, Scientology is protecting the home, the church, the family, decent morals... positively no wife swapping. It's a dirty Communist trick ... national boundaries,

the concepts of RIGHT and WRONG against evil free thinking psychiatrist) can hardly recommend him to the militant students. Certainly it is time for the Scientologists to come out in plain English on one side or the other, if they expect the trust and support of young people. Which side are you on Hubbard, which side are you on?"

"The Electronic Revolution" explores Burroughs' thoughts on cameras and tape recorders, taking cut-ups off the page and into the real world. Of course, Hubbard's reactive mind is central to the essay. Still, though, his attitude towards Hubbard is a little sour. Without being outright offensive, Burroughs takes a few cheap shots:

"Ron Hubbard, founder of Scientology, says that certain words and word combinations can produce serious illnesses and mental disturbances. I can claim some skill in the scrivener's trade, but I cannot guarantee to write a passage that will make someone physically ill. If Mr. Hubbard's claim is justified, this is certainly a matter for further research, and we can easily find out experimentally whether his claim is justified or not."

Although his tone is sarcastic, Burroughs goes on to suggest that experiments would prove Hubbard right to some extent. Indeed, Hubbard claimed to know of words and phrases that would literally harm the reader or listener. In Burroughs' copy of Hubbard's "Standard Dianetic Gains" he underlined material related to this idea, wherein Hubbard describes an attempt by "three or four criminal types" to steal high-level Scientology materials. The criminals "experienced no change whatever where they tried to use them." However, "in some cases... these same materials carelessly viewed would produce heavy physical reactions."

He goes on to describe more of his ideas about engrams and the reactive mind, invoking Hubbard's claim that opposing phrases are used to elicit reactions. He speculates that with electronic innovations, it is becoming easier to utilize the reactive mind for mass control. Burroughs concludes: "The RM is a built-in electronic police force armed with hideous threats." Soon he is tying in the Mayan calendar, Korzybski, and hieroglyphics. It is evident by this stage, if not before, that the reactive mind tied everything together for Burroughs. It made sense of his other obsessions. It lent them legitimacy, and made it possible for Burroughs to explain them in relatively simple terms. Again, throughout the essay Burroughs' reliance on Hubbard's theories to put forth his own ideas implies that Burroughs was fond of Hubbard, or actively engaged in Scientology, but this essay, too, ends with negativity. "Mr. Hubbard says that Scientology is a game where everybody wins. There are no games where everybody wins."

Burroughs was enraged when his publishers neglected to send out any review copies of his book, and only a reviewer for *The Guardian* picked up a copy and wrote about it. Although the review was generally favorable, Burroughs was offended that the reviewer mocked his championing of odd ideas. It said, "Mr. Burroughs is barmy and possibly paranoid like his hero Reich whom he believes was *driven* into paranoia..." Indeed, whilst an entertaining book, Burroughs does come across as a paranoid kook, not unlike the man who had invented the orgone accumulator. Furthermore, to these accusations of paranoia, he ascribed some great conspiracy, concluding that nobody would review his book because of threats from Scientologists.

That year, Burroughs also worked on the stories, "The Discipline of DE" and "Bay of Pigs," both of which concern Scientology to some degree. "The Discipline of DE" (DE stands for "do easy") has been described as "Buddhist noir" and is said to be one of Burroughs' forays into Zen, but reading it in the light of his interest in Scientology, it is clearly a satire of Hubbard's writing and, to an extent, his ideas. The language alone tells us that this is not Burroughs' own voice. The simple, jovial instruction,

172

intended to make everything sound terribly easy, is an attempt to mimic Hubbard, whose books are purposefully accessible and attempt to make his methods sound phenomenally easy. DE, like Scientology, makes a lot of astounding promises, and students can expect to achieve many of the same benefits of becoming a clear in Scientology:

> "You know your entire past history just what year month day and hour everything happened. If you have heard a language for any length of time you know that language. You have a computer in your brain. DE will show you how to use it."

When Burroughs repeatedly talks about "advancing" in DE, or starting over after making a mistake, he is using Hubbard's language and his ideas. Moreover, there are references to "present time" – one of Hubbard's ideas from *Dianetics*, in which Burroughs had frequently shown interest. DE seems to be based upon Hubbard's idea of "mocking up" situations, essentially visualizing them and running them to remove negative connotations in the mind. This is done with pictures rather than words. Burroughs says that DE is a method of disconnecting from the reactive mind. The title is another clue, as Scientologese makes liberal use of acronyms.

"Bay of Pigs" contains fewer references to Scientology, but one of the characters, representing an organization called "The Academy" describes the group's training methods. The methods outlined are similar to those advocated by Burroughs in his *Mayfair* Academy series, and include Scientology, karate, and aikido. There is also a reference to the trauma of birth, which was a preoccupation of Hubbard's. Interestingly, the story describes the abuse Burroughs suffered from A.J. O'Connell prior to enrolling at the Los Alamos Ranch School, suggesting that the Academy helps people deal with such issues. Naturally, Burroughs also includes the Mayans, whose knowledge the evil government forces of the world are seeking, and whom the Academy seeks to protect.

In 1970 Burroughs began collaborating with Malcolm McNeill, the artist with whom he produced a comic strip for *Cyclops* magazine, called "The Unspeakable Mr. Hart." Burroughs' text for the comic (which ran to only six hundred words) began, "Mr. L. Ron Hubbard has postulated a Reactive Mind..." and went on to concern the Mayans, viruses, and tape recorders. McNeill and Burroughs began expanding the project into a book called *Ah Pook is Here*, but the process was a comedy of errors and it wasn't published until 1979, when the book was released with only Burroughs' text.[8] Working on the comic strip, Burroughs and McNeill had never actually met, but during their first meeting, at Burroughs' Duke Street flat in 1970, he explained to McNeill that the story was as much about the reactive mind as anything else. McNeill spent time with Burroughs, and was introduced to John McMaster, who seems to have been a fairly regular visitor during the seventies. McMaster claimed that the Scientologists were trying to kill him, and then introduced McNeill to the E-meter, auditing the artist for half an hour with questions such as "What is a condition of existence? What is not a condition of existence?" and "Who is someone you have known? Who is someone you have not known?" Later, McNeill dropped acid and claimed to have seen inside the reactive mind.

In late October Burroughs' paranoia was on display in a letter to Charles Upton. He also indicated a move away from Hubbard's processing ideas. By then he believed that the reactive mind was planted in the human brain by a powerful collective who were apparently backing Hubbard. It existed then as a method of control, and Scientology was no longer a means to resist control.

> "My contention is that whoever is behind Hubbard planted it in the first place, like say somebody introduces malaria into an area and when everyone's ass is dragging the ground enter the savior with quinine. Oh not too much and only

---

8 It was released by John Calder as part of a collection. In 2012, McNeill released the artwork originally produced for the project as a stand-alone graphic novel. Burroughs' text was not included.

to be given out to the obedient ones who scream out 'Thank You Ron' at every opportunity. I have rarely read any thing as disgusting as the praise lavished on this old con man by his followers."

Still, he considers the reactive mind a real thing and suggests the methods of an alternative group – the Association of International Dianologists. He seems to think this group would be superior as they lack the severity of discipline possessed by the Church of Scientology. He proceeds to repeat his claim about Hubbard's theft of ideas, and brings up the CIA once again:

"A highly placed scientologist admitted to me that the CIA has this material. Therefore I think it should be freely circulated among any militant groups or any students of control systems with a view to deactivating its effectiveness."

One major interest of Burroughs' at the time was Hubbard's claim that certain materials could make a person go insane. Thus, Burroughs distributed these materials among his friends and was pleased to find that none of them got sick or lost their minds. He concluded, then, that the reason Hubbard didn't want his confidential materials made public was that they contained stolen information. Indeed, Hubbard did utilize other writers' work without credit. He was also known for entering lawsuits "at the drop of a hat," but Burroughs felt that he had the right to publish these works because, he quipped, "Hubbard claims the material is millions of years old so we may assume it is now in the public domain."

On October 20th, a year after Kerouac died, Burroughs' mother, Laura, passed away in her nursing home. Burroughs was immediately filled with shame. He had promised his mother that he would never leave her alone, especially when she was old and frail, and yet for the last years of her life, while she suffered and lost her mind, he didn't visit. He had come to the United States several times (including a visit only months prior to Laura's death), but never made the effort to see her. As with his son, he had sent cards and letters instead of actually visiting. It was just another in a lifelong list of failures as a family man. The freedom to travel and to write had taken a terrible toll.

In late 1970 Burroughs made a habit of cutting out stories about Scientology from British newspapers, possibly as research for another essay. He would sometimes use these news clippings for cutting up or mashing together in art projects. They came from different sources, as Burroughs read a lot of newspapers, but one of the running themes through the latter half of the year was related to Geoffrey Johnson MP, who was being sued for libel by the Church of Scientology after appearing on the BBC show, *24 Hours*, to voice his concerns over their actions. Burroughs, now fascinated by scandals involving the Church, cut out articles containing any reference to this case.

On November 29th, Burroughs wrote about a dream in which Hubbard had died, and Burroughs was invited to his funeral. He notes that it was not well attended, and that the casket "seems too small to accommodate his big fat carcass." He says, "There he is looking as if he were alone and had just sold the widow a fraudulent peach orchard."[9] Despite the old man being dead in a box, Burroughs has nothing nice to say. References are made to Jack Parsons, a friend with whom Hubbard explored the occult world of Aleister Crowley, and to Rachmaninoff, whose music Hubbard supposedly enjoyed – at least according to the *Sunday Times* article Burroughs read in 1969, about Hubbard's links to Crowley. He describes Hubbard's life as a "tissue of lies and false degrees," referring to notorious claims about his education, and says that all his successes were sudden and unwarranted. "I remember the fear that crawled out of his slimy con man voice," he says, before realizing that Hubbard is actually alive – even his death was a fake. When Burroughs later cut up the text, he described Hubbard as "looking as if he were a black panther."

---

9 This might be a reference to the con men down in Texas who made a living from selling bad land to people like Burroughs. The expression is repeated in "Immortality" from his collection, *The Adding Machine,* and also in *The Place of Dead Roads*. He uses it again to describe Hubbard in his collection of correspondence, *Rub Out the Words.*

The December issue of *Mayfair* was Burroughs' last, the end of a long and fruitful collaboration. The last words Burroughs spoke to his editor, Graham Masterton, were, "Every time in recorded history that somebody has invented something that helps to set people free, somebody else will quickly come along and take control of it, and turn it into an instrument of oppression and control." He had begun his relationship with *Mayfair* as a curious man, whose cynicism was put aside in search of a cure he desperately needed. He was taken in by the Scientologists and they convinced him they had fixed him, and he heaped unabashed praise upon them. Yet two years later, Burroughs is spitting vitriol every which way, attempting to tarnish any lingering shred of credibility the Church may have had, seemingly unaware that he had been permanently changed. Hubbard's teachings had merged with Burroughs' own ideas, working with Korzybski and Reich, applying themselves to his perceptions of the world, and had become an inextricable part of his outlook.

At the beginning of 1971, there was a great deal of interest in a film version of *Naked Lunch*. Burroughs had clearly become interested in the potentialities of film over the previous few years, and with Gysin and Balch he had looked into the possibility of making his masterpiece a movie. In the early seventies, Balch, Gysin, and Burroughs formed a company called Friendly Films to produce the movie, with the screenplay written by Gysin. Although Burroughs hated Gysin's script, such was his respect for the man himself that he went along with the project nonetheless. In May, 1971, Mick Jagger visited Burroughs' flat to discuss starring in the movie, but ultimately he was unhappy with Balch as a director, and Burroughs could see that the project was doomed.[10] On August 28th, Balch and Gysin approached Dennis Hopper, whose movie, *Easy Rider*, Burroughs greatly enjoyed, and attempted to convince him to star in the movie, but they were unsuccessful. Later, Burroughs claimed that James Taylor was attached, and that they were set to shoot in October. By the middle of 1972, Gysin was giving interviews in which he

10 When Burroughs wrote to his son about the project, he claimed to have enjoyed Gysin's script, and said only that Jagger was too busy to be in the film, although he was likely trying to put a positive spin on things.

claimed the movie was all but ready to start shooting, although ultimately no movie version was made until David Cronenberg's 1991 adaptation.

In May 1971, Burroughs wrote an angry letter to the British headquarters of Scientology. This time it was related to money he believed he was owed. Back in spring, 1968, during his time at Saint Hill, Burroughs was supposedly charged $75 for a course that he claimed not to have taken, and which indeed is absent from records of his time with the Church. In the intervening three years, Burroughs had sent numerous requests to have his money reimbursed, but his letters had gone ignored. Although his public tirades against the religion had gained the attention of its most prominent figures, he was evidently lacking the clout to obtain a small reimbursement.

Still thoroughly enraged with Scientology, Burroughs wrote a short story called "Ali's Smile." This may have been intended for publication in *The Wild Boys*, which featured a number of loosely similar chapters with the word "smile" in the title. The story was published in 1971 in an extremely limited run of ninety-nine copies, each with a recording of Burroughs reading his story, and then reprinted in a much larger printing in 1973. That same year, it was also included in Burroughs' collection, *Exterminator!* Like the early chapters of *The Wild Boys*, "Ali's Smile" opens like a screenplay: "The set is a country house"; "The camera moves at a purposeful trot." The story is scattered and odd, like so many of Burroughs', playing around with time and space. It is inspired by his time at Saint Hill, but is entirely indicative of his views on Scientology circa 1970-71.

The story is set in an English town, clearly inspired by East Grinstead, where Saint Hill was located. Reference is made to "Ye Old Bramble Tyme Motel," which is based upon the Brambletie Hotel where Burroughs stayed early in his Scientology training. The main character is a retired colonial officer called Clinch Smith, who receives a letter from a Scientologist friend called Harry, filled with Scientologese: "Your flippant attitude towards Scientology makes you a downstate suppressive person. I disconnect from you. Don't ever get on my comlines again."[11] Stories about Scientologists "disconnecting" from friends and family were common in newspapers, and Burroughs had cut out and collected some such articles, probably with the intent of researching this story. Depressed, Smith looks at a kris[12] hanging on his wall and remembers a boy named Ali. Smith had found Ali dancing under a curse in a market in Malay. He rescued the boy, but Ali soon returned to the market and began killing people with the kris. Smith had to shoot Ali in order to stop the rampage. Back in the present, Smith takes the kris and makes his way towards the Scientology Center, but ends up at a local market, where he finds there is a riot. A group of hippies is fighting some locals, and there are members of Scientology's Sea Org littered around. Smith stabs a man named Lord Westfield, who, in a strange sequence, hires a private detective to infiltrate the Church of Scientology, along with several others. He is eventually shot dead, but the fight continues until a giant slag heap collapses and covers the town. The "ghost face of Ali" smiles in the black sky over the destruction.

In a bizarre passage, Burroughs describes "The Scientologist… whose name was Reg," who had sent the letter announcing his severing of ties with Clinch Smith. It is not clear why these two paragraphs are included, as his purpose in the story is otherwise limited to that of a device – the writer of the insulting letter that sends Smith on a murder spree. But for Burroughs it was important to cram as much Scientology into the story as possible, and so we have a little about Reg before the story cuts – again quite randomly – to Lord Westfield and his private investigator.

> "The Scientologist, meanwhile, whose name was
> Reg, walked away in a down-stat condition. He
> could feel his gains ebbing away in the afternoon
> streets that were suddenly full of raw menace…

---

11 "Downstate" is a mistake. Burroughs probably meant "downstat," referring to people who are not doing well in a Scientological way. "Comlines" is also a typo. He was referring to "comm lines" – an imaginary line between two people who are talking.

12 Kris - a dagger from Southeast Asia

> The arc was flowing out of him and he felt a
> terrible weakness. He feared the sin of self-
> invalidation.
> "'I must up-stat myself,' he told himself, firmly.
> 'I'll make a report to Ethics.' ... He turned a
> corner, and there, just ahead, a knot of people.
> Accident, fight perhaps, here was a chance to
> prove himself. Perhaps he could save a little girl
> from dying of burns with a brilliant touch-assist.
> The words of Ron came back to him: 'in any
> emergency, just be there, saying firmly, 'You are
> in my space.'"

One gets the feeling Burroughs is showing off. It is unlikely
many of his readers would understand the language above,
which is probably intentional in this case. In the past Burroughs
had littered his writing with Scientologese but now he is clearly
mocking such language by making the references even more
obscure. He is attempting to highlight the silliness of Scientology,
and the level of indoctrination experienced by its members. Later
in the passage, Burroughs even sneaks in the word "wog," which
was one of his favored weapons for attacking the Church.

Soon we are following Lord Westfield, who has hired a
detective from a firm called Jenkins and Coldbourne. "Get me
the data on Scientology," he tells them. The detective shows
Westfield a stack of pamphlets, but Westfield balks. He demands
his detective enroll in a course, returning each day to run through
the lessons and auditing with Westfield.

The detective is reluctant, as he, too, has experience with
Scientology.

> "They'll smell me out on the E-meter, if you'll
> pardon the expression, Sir; they have this lie-
> detector, Sir. You can't beat it, Sir. You see I did
> a job for them once... my wife took a personal
> efficiency course at the London Center and that's
> how I got into it... and this grim old biddy drags

me into a broomcloset, puts me on the cans, and says I should have told her anything I didn't."

This statement suggests that the detective character may have been based upon Burroughs himself. The line "grim old biddy" was used by Burroughs to describe the woman who audited him, and he was audited in a broom closet because the other rooms were filled. He also refers to the E-meter electrodes as "cans." Note also the repeated use of "sir," which harkens back to an earlier description of Scientology from a Nova Police cadet in *Nova Express*. He goes on to make reference to grey rags tied around the arm, having to petition other members for forgiveness after being late, dreading the Sec Check, and the back-stabbing atmosphere among his fellow Scientologists. These are clear references to Burroughs' experiences at Saint Hill.

Burroughs moved briefly into teaching in late 1971, after being invited to Switzerland by Al de Grazia,[13] who had opened an institution called the University of the New World. The school was meant to be progressive and offer an alternative style of education, which appealed to Burroughs, who'd spent most of the sixties attempting to educate the world about the Burroughs Academy through his writing. He had even toyed with the idea of opening an actual school and teaching things like Scientology, death rays, and karate.[14] Alas, the University of the New World was a run-down resort for hippies and drop-outs. It was badly organized and he lamented that there was no rigid structure in place, which he considered necessary in any form of education. Upon arrival it became obvious he would not be paid, the school was under police surveillance, and his classes were filled with idiots. The altitude made him sick, too. He was asked to teach "creative writing," which he found difficult because he wasn't <u>sure that writing</u> could be taught at all. It wasn't all bad, though,

13 Brother of the Ed de Grazia, the lawyer who defended *Naked Lunch*.
14 In a 1974 interview with *Rolling Stone* (in which Burroughs interviewed David Bowie) Burroughs claimed that he was working on "an institute of advanced studies somewhere in Scotland," and in a letter to Allen Ginsberg in the same year he contemplated hosting it at Ginsberg's Cherry Farm property, saying, "I am convinced that America is the place to set up such a center."

as the university eventually paid for his travel, his hotel was very comfortable, and he found a student who was interested in learning how to use the E-meter.

After Switzerland, Burroughs travelled to Los Angeles to talk more about a film version of *Naked Lunch*, but the very next day the project died, and Burroughs took off for New York. Here, he enjoyed some pornographic gay cinema, and worried about how *The Wild Boys* would sell with that for competition. His book came out in October 1971, and he briefly looked into the possibility of a *Wild Boys* porno, but that, too, failed as the screenplay he wrote would have been too expensive to produce.[15] In 1968 he had enjoyed these movies and wrote to Balch about cutting them up, but now he was depressed. He looked forward to a return to London, but when he got back he was still unhappy. By this time he hated everything about London, repeating the pattern that had dragged him around the world, via Mexico City, Tangier, and Paris. He wrote his son to say, "England is a gloomy cold unlighted sinking ship that will disappear with a spectral cough."

One element of Scientology that is conspicuously absent from Burroughs' letters and writings, but which is widely known today, are the stories of Xenu, dictator of the Galactic Confederacy. In Operating Thetan Level III, an extremely advanced stage in Scientology training, these stories are related by Hubbard. Known as "Incident II" within the Church, these confidential materials are only available to members who have paid thousands of dollars for the privilege, and Church spokespeople have avoided making reference to them. The story of Xenu bringing billions of beings to earth, gathering them around a volcano, and killing them with hydrogen bombs is what Hubbard called a "space opera," and has been the subject of ridicule ever since being leaked to the public. Hubbard wrote the material in late 1966, and recorded it as a taped lecture in September, 1967, for study by Scientologists. Its absence in Burroughs' letters and other writings is likely due to the fact that Burroughs was simply

---

15 In talks with the producer, Fred Halsted, Burroughs suggested various ways of making the text easier to film, and suggested having the Wild Boys use E-meters.

unaware of this aspect of Scientology. Having never reached the level of Operating Thetan, he would not have been exposed to this information, and it was only 1969 that references began appearing in the press.

In October 1971, Burroughs was so at odds with the Church of Scientology that he even brought Xenu into his assault, and in a letter to John Cooke he mocks Hubbard's "third rate science fiction."[16] He outright dismissed the possibility of the Galactic Confederacy and Xenu, but again showed faith in Hubbard's fundamental notion. The story of Xenu tells the story of the origin of thetans, which Burroughs noted was similar to ideas put down by other thinkers. Rather than again accusing Hubbard of intellectual theft, he suggests further study. His idea of further study involves the E-meter, in which he evidently had a renewed interest. Still, he ended the letter by asking Cooke about the R2-45 procedure – another relatively new scandal for the Church.[17] Burroughs hoped that Cooke had information about R2-45, which was first suggested by Hubbard in 1952, back when Cooke was with the Church, but Cooke claimed to know nothing. Burroughs called him a "worthless bastard," and said, "I *know* he knows these commands."

In London, Burroughs started work on *Port of Saints*, a sequel to *The Wild Boys*, and began assembling a collection called *Exterminator!*, which would be published by Viking Press in mid-1972. He took up with a new lover, with a personality similar to Jack Anderson, who talked in his sleep. Burroughs viewed these bits of speech as natural cut-ups, and noted them down. But he was miserable. His boyfriend was violent and difficult to be around, and every time he left his dingy little flat,

---

16 Burroughs was referring to official Church doctrine, rather than the books Hubbard admitted were fiction – his early sci-fi novels. Incidentally, Burroughs had been reading a lot of science fiction in the late sixties and early seventies, and was reading Frank Herbert's *Dune* that October. He had high regard for writers who could produce believable science fiction.

17 R2-45 is an "auditing process" advocated by Hubbard that involves the use of a gun (a Colt .45) to execute a person, thereby releasing their thetan. Burroughs also uses the phrase 'fair game,' which is another of Hubbard's terms, meaning that any and all means necessary can be used to silence or punish a perceived enemy of Scientology.

he felt that people were insulting him. He took to practicing curses on those who displeased him, and one of these was an establishment called the Moka Bar, where he had been treated with disrespect, and had gotten sick from the food. Using his guerrilla tactics, he made tape recordings and took photos, then cut these with materials obtained elsewhere in order to displace the Moka Bar in time. A few months later, the business shut down and Burroughs was convinced that his curse had hit its mark.

> "I have frequently observed that this simple operation – making recordings and taking pictures of some location you wish to discommode or destroy, then playing recordings back and taking more pictures – will result in accidents, fires, removals, especially the latter."

Another target of Burroughs' was the Scientology Center at 37 Fitzroy Street. He attempted the same strategy of attack as with the Moka Bar, and a few months later they moved to a new building. Again, Burroughs was convinced that his curse had worked, and failed to entertain the idea that maybe they'd moved to a better location. He later attempted the same trick at their new premises but was unsuccessful. In fact, forty years later they are still there.

In January, *Rolling Stone* sent Rob Palmer and Charles Gatewood to visit Burroughs in London for a feature story. Off the record, Burroughs told Palmer and Gatewood that it was Gysin who introduced him to Scientology, and remarked. "Brion's a prankster... got me hooked on Scientology, nasty man. Should I thank Brion – or should I kill him? Let's ask the E-meter." When he sat down and demonstrated for his visitors the function of the E-meter (asking himself "Am I me?" and "Am I that I am?") Gatewood snapped the photo that's on the cover of this book.

When the interview began, Burroughs was eager to start talking about the E-meter. He begins by describing it as "a sort of sloppy form of electrical brain stimulation," and goes through some of the questions – "What are you willing to talk about?

What would you like to tell me about that?" Then he talks about it in relation to control, and its possible misuse:

> "It seems to me that the best insurance that the discovery is not used for control purposes is people knowing about it. The more people know about it, the less chance there is to monopolize it, particularly such very simple techniques as these…"

He goes on to describe some of its more practical applications:

> "Now the E-meter is in fact a lie-detector and a mind-reading machine. You can read anyone's mind with it – but not the content, only the reactions. But if I ask a specific question, say if I ask someone, 'Did you fuck your mother? Did you fuck your mother?' I'll get a read. That's a protest read, maybe dreams, fantasies. But if after going through all that, it still reads, by God, he did. I mean there's no reading a lie detector on a direct question like that.
>
> "Now there are many actions you can get on this needle, but the commonest is a fall, which indicates a reaction. A fall is only one reaction, there are others. There's a rise, which means boredom, inattention. There's also a floating needle, which is a point of release, which is the scientology processing aims for. The needle floats back and forth, quite free.
>
> "If you've got a business associate and you get a strong read on his name, you're much more suspicious of him than you may realize, and usually with good reason. Any incident that disturbs you, if you run it to a floating needle, it sort of evaporates. I use it sometimes for that, not very much anymore, but it works, very well.

> If some disturbing incident has just happened,
> you run it on there until you get a floating needle.
> It may take varying lengths of time, usually not
> more than ten or 15 minutes at the most. A floating
> needle means that it's gone for now. It may come
> back; it may disturb you tomorrow."

After talking about the device, Burroughs goes on to the usual subjects: apomorphine, the Mayans, viruses, government suppression of various breakthroughs, weaponry, and drugs. They talk about the Burroughs Academy from his *Mayfair* column, and about his time in Switzerland. Palmer asks Burroughs whether he would include elements of Eastern philosophy and Burroughs says no, because although there may be some value in these practices, the West is simply too far ahead. "Their statistics are not all that good," he says of India in particular. He cites "electrical brain stimulation" as an example of Western superiority, referring to the E-meter, or to the potentialities of the E-meter in his own opinion. He references Hubbard again in relation to education, saying that were he to open a Burroughs Academy, he would have his students perform "dummy situations," referring to the process of mocking up tasks.

In 1972, Burroughs collaborated with Balch on a short film called *Bill and Tony*. It begins with Burroughs and Balch swapping names, and then moves on to a shot of Burroughs' floating head reciting information about the Scientology process of exteriorization. Later this is repeated in Balch's voice. The information is taken more or less from a Scientology auditing manual. As part of his studying, Burroughs copied and paraphrased Scientology texts, and this probably accounts for the slight differences between his speech and the actual text.

On April 24th, 1972, Maurice Girodias, the man who had first published *Naked Lunch*, wrote to Burroughs about a forthcoming book – *Inside Scientology: How I Joined Scientology and Became Superhuman* by Robert Kaufman. It was a daring exposé by a high level defector, and it was going to create a storm. Girodias had always been attracted to controversial publications, but he probably didn't realize just what he was getting into with the Church of Scientology. By the time he wrote to Burroughs, Kaufman had been threatened by the Church, had the phone lines to his house cut, had part of his manuscript stolen, had another part stolen from the printers' offices, and finally the Church filed for injunctions to stop publication in New York, Boston, and London. After publication, Girodias and Kaufman were sued by the Church, who kept up their illegal assaults, eventually costing Girodias huge sums of money. In Canada, the Church of Scientology attempted to sue libraries and bookstores which stocked the book. They even managed to enact a boycott of a piano recital by Kaufman, resulting in the author playing to an empty concert hall. The FBI eventually turned up documents relating to the incident, which the Church called the "Carnegie Hall Incident."

What Girodias wanted from Burroughs was a review of Kaufman's book, which Burroughs was delighted to produce. He wrote back on June 18th, referring to Scientologists as "those bastards," and said, referring to the harassment of Kaufman and Olympia Press, "It is certainly time that such tactics were exposed." However, rather than a review, he took the opening as another chance to launch an attack on Scientology in the October 26th issue of *Rolling Stone*. In fact, the piece starts like a review:

> "The upper levels of Scientology processing are classified as 'confidential,' which means that only those who have completed the lower grades, passed security checks, and paid the large fees in advance are allowed to see and run this material. The most drastic penalties are invoked against those who reveal these materials. Mr. Kaufman has shown real courage in publishing Hubbard's so-called confidential materials for the first time in *Inside Scientology*. Step right up, here it is. This is what Scientologists pay $10,000 to see."

However, soon it becomes apparent that the space *Rolling Stone* has given him will be used for his own exposé. He launches into a history of his own attacks on Hubbard, reiterating his stance on the use of the word "wog," and Hubbard's unwillingness to share information with other sectors. He mentions being put in a Condition of Treason, although he erroneously states that it was due to one of his *Mayfair* articles.[18] One major difference in Burroughs' thinking is that he now appears aware that Scientology was a money-making operation. Earlier he seemed unsure of why Hubbard wouldn't allowed outsiders to view his secrets, but finally, after reading Kaufman's book, Burroughs can attack Hubbard for trying to turn a quick profit. With the detachment of several years away from his intensive studies, Burroughs is wittier and more scathing. His use of sarcasm throughout isn't unique, but his clarity of thought makes each blow hit harder. Despite being labeled a review, this is one of his finest assaults on Scientology.

After acknowledging that Scientology has some positive qualities, Burroughs moves on to provide some glimpses of his time at Saint Hill. For this he went back to his unpublished notes and took some lines and ideas, and embellished the experience to make it sound more exciting, giving the operation a decidedly military feel. He focuses on the fear of failing to impress, of Sec Checks and the Joberg. He implies that Hubbard is calling for executions when he says, "Any Sea Org member contacting [a group of suppressives] is to run R-2-45." He explores the paranoia and repeats his joke about the vending machine being in a "Condition of Liability." In an early version of his review, he mocked the clearing course as "a spat of idiotic contradictory commands," giving examples such as "to be animals to be me to stay present to be you," and so forth, although this was removed from the published version that appeared in *Rolling Stone*. Again he brings up the CIA, which had become an obsession of his in recent years. He compares the E-meter to a CIA device, and his auditor to an agent. He now seems more aware of the methods of control:

18 He acknowledged in a follow up piece that he was excommunicated prior to the offending *Mayfair* article.

188

"Scientology is a model control system, a state in fact with its own courts, police, rewards and penalties. It is based on a tight ingroup like the CIA, Islam, the Mormons, etc. Inside are the Rights with the Truth. Outside are the Commies, the Infidels, the Unfaithful, the Suppressives."

Burroughs ends by chastising Scientologists for their attacks on Kaufman and Girodias, and then suggesting once again that Hubbard's ideas – this time his methods of control, rather than resisting control – warrant further study.

Overall, Burroughs' so-called review is one of his finer pieces of writing on the subject of Scientology. Despite hardly even referencing the book, he poses logical arguments with a cutting wit, and recounts some artfully absurd stories from his own time within the religion. Clearly the distance between him and Saint Hill has allowed for a greater clarity of thought, and it seems that he has put aside the things he learned in order to focus entirely on discrediting Hubbard. His concessions are minimal. The most positive thing he says is that Scientology "does produce certain effects," and "merits serious study." These comments, though, are drowned out by his attacks.

In early December, someone named R. Sorrell at Saint Hill Manor wrote to *Rolling Stone* with a list of corrections in relation to Burroughs' review, marking the beginning of a second round of public debates between Burroughs and the Church. His aim was "to show that Mr. Burroughs may be a writer but cannot always be trusted to be an accurate one."

Burroughs wrote back, taking Sorrell point-for-point. The first point was that the Sec Checks, to which Burroughs continuously alluded in his writings on Scientology, were scrapped in 1968, shortly after Burroughs left the Church. Burroughs replied by saying that he was aware of this, and indeed he had been aware of it since the announcement was made, but that didn't stop him from writing about it deliberately as though they were still common practice.

Later, to Sorrell's claim that "The Church of Scientology is a non-profit organization. L. Ron Hubbard does not make any money from it," Burroughs replied:

> "I have listed some of the assets from the church. Mr. Hubbard has boats, villas, manors at his disposal. I submit that he profits from this non profit organization. If he is not a rich man, he certainly lives like one."

To the argument that Scientologists do not use words like "wog," unless describing "a person like Mr. Burroughs whose unwillingness to be honest has led him to spy on a church," Burroughs replied:

> "I have heard Mr. Hubbard use the term Wog on taped lectures. I have heard him define the term as a 'Worthy Oriental Gentleman.' I have seen bulletins that speak of the Wog World and Wog Law. As is well known, the term Wog has come to mean Non White. Mr. Sorrell could see it being used to describe a person like Mr. Burroughs? Thank you for that, Mr. Sorrell. I should be glad to change a color that has disgraced itself from the Conquistadors to Hiroshima. To spy on a church? I am not religious, Mr. Sorrell. I find it impossible to communicate with anyone that is religious. Whether the religion is Communism, Catholicism, or Scientology. They all have the answers. Facts are irrelevant. When I found out that Scientology is a religion that has nothing to do with scientific research on a subject that interests me, I withdrew."

Most interestingly, to the accusation made in Burroughs' review that "Scientology is a model control system," Sorrell says, "Mr. Burroughs has it arse about face. Scientology reveals

the control system; seeing what it is you are then free from it."
Burroughs replied: "An organized Church is a control system
by its hierarchical nature." Despite his belief in gods and the
possibility of an afterlife, Burroughs had never subscribed to
organized religion, yet he had failed for a long time to perceive
that Scientology was such a rigid system.

The *Rolling Stone* correspondence (comprised of Burroughs'
review, Sorrell's reply, and Burroughs' final reply) make up the
second of two public battles, the first being his war of words on
the pages of *Mayfair*. From the first battle, his original statement
("I, William S. Burroughs, Challenge You, L. Ron Hubbard") and
his "Open Letter to Gorden Mustain" were collected in a book
on Scientology, called *Ali's Smile/Naked Scientology*, published
in 1978. Also included were the *Rolling Stone* materials and the
short story, "Ali's Smile."

In early 1973, Burroughs was interviewed by *Gay Sunshine*,
a magazine for homosexuals. One of his interviewers had been
through auditing and had a fairly negative view of Scientology.
Throughout the interview, Burroughs demonstrates a lingering
interest in the E-meter and related technologies, but overall his
tone is disparaging:

> "Scientology *is* a religion. They call it a religion.
> When I found it out it was a religion, I quit.
> I'm not interested in religions. The whole thing
> in Scientology is this instrument called the
> E-meter..."

He describes the device at length, and then his interviewer asks
whether his opinions regarding the reactive mind still remain.

> "Ron Hubbard's concept of the reactive mind,
> I don't hold with it at all. Of course, it's partly
> what Freud called the unconscious."

It's interesting that Burroughs claimed to be no longer interested
in Hubbard's reactive mind, as the concept does continue to

appear in his work throughout the remainder of his life. Indeed, even minutes after making that claim, he is reading an essay to his interviewer, which contains the idea of "removing" specific memories from the mind. Regardless of his conscious choices, Hubbard's theories were thoroughly embedded in Burroughs' mind.

Shortly after his public disavowal of the reactive mind, Burroughs claimed once again that he was finished with the E-meter. He told Eric Mottram, who was interviewing him for *Snack* magazine, "With further use of the E-meter I'm not at all sure that it isn't quite valueless." He explains that recent research suggested that technology like the E-meter may interfere with the brain's ability to learn. Additionally, he claims that a floating needle, whilst pleasurable, is short-lived. He compares it to acupuncture.

In August, Burroughs continued his psychic exploration with a course called Mind Dimensions. It was run by a WWII veteran called Bruce McManaway who could reputedly heal with his hands, and claimed to have been used by the navy to detect enemy submarines in the Atlantic. Naturally, this sort of thing interested Burroughs, but when McManaway said that a group of people practicing his method could lift a grand piano with their minds, Burroughs replied, "I'm from the 'show-me-state' and I'd sure like to see it." That he had learned from his experiences with Scientology is rather unlikely, as Burroughs always considered himself a bit of a skeptic, despite substantial evidence to the contrary.

Throughout much of 1973, Burroughs was also reading Robert A. Monroe's *Journeys Out of the Body*, as part of his continued "psychic research." He recommended it in several letters to friends, saying, "This book points the way to the future as I see it." The book is about leaving the body and travelling, and the author's bizarre stories are not entirely dissimilar to L. Ron Hubbard's. It should also be noted that Burroughs was always fascinated by the Scientology process of exteriorization, which appears similar in its purported results, although achieved by very different means, to Monroe's account. The book also contained references to the possibility of telepathy, as did Sheila Ostrander's *Psychic Discoveries Behind the Iron* Curtain, which Burroughs also greatly enjoyed.

Burroughs was desperate to leave England, but he had little money (as his books were not selling well), nowhere with any definite prospects, and increasingly he was tied down by the huge boxes of writing that he had collected. He was sending cash to his son, whose marriage had broken up and whose life was still a mess, and was looking for a new country – with Ireland, Scotland, and Costa Rica top of his list. Brion Gysin suggested selling his archives, and found a buyer in Lichtenstein who would pay cash.[19] He spent around six months compiling his archives, with help from Barry Miles. In November, thanks to Allen Ginsberg, Burroughs was invited to work as a teacher at New York City College.

Burroughs had been an expat for twenty-four years, but finally, at the age of sixty, he was returning to the United States. Leaving England around Christmas, Burroughs began teaching in February and worked until May, earning a significant amount of money for his efforts. He found New York enjoyable (although every time he moved to a new place he seemed to focus largely on its positive attributes), and just like his previous stay, he was honored to find himself adored by young readers. He felt that New York was about the only place in the world that improved with each passing year, although he wasn't overly enthusiastic about teaching. Half his students expected him to be like a character from *Naked Lunch*, and the other half had no idea who he was, and in any case, they barely looked up from their comic books to see.

It was in New York, whilst teaching at the City College, that Burroughs met James Grauerholz – the man who would remain his friend and manager for the rest of his life, and who, after Burroughs' death in 1997, would become his literary executor. This was the first person willing to entirely devote his life to Burroughs. It was Ginsberg who introduced the twenty-one year old Beat-enthusiast to Burroughs, suggesting that Grauerholz

19 These were known as the Vaduz archives, and are now held in the New York Public Library, accessible to researchers.

become his secretary. Soon after meeting, Burroughs decided that he wanted something more, and they very briefly became lovers. Soon, though, they transitioned to friendship, and Grauerholz began to run Burroughs' life for him as Burroughs wrote.

When he finished up at City College, the University of Buffalo offered him $15,000 to teach, but he was tired of teaching. Besides, Grauerholz had introduced him to the world of readings. He could make as much as a thousand dollars just reading from his books on stage, without being tied down or forced to lecture ungrateful, apathetic students. He put a lot of effort into preparing his readings, thinking of them as performances rather than lectures, and he was a hit. Over the next ten years he performed around a hundred and fifty times, making a respectable amount of cash.

He returned to London briefly because he hadn't expected his stint in New York to be permanent, and had things that needed brought over. Upon his return he moved into a bigger apartment and had an orgone accumulator built by a friend. "Maybe I'm as crazy as Reich was," he said, "but I do think there is something here."

In early 1974, Burroughs was interviewed by *The Anchor*, and throughout the interview his views sound somewhat inspired by Scientology. He criticizes psychiatry, suggesting that a person needn't examine the cause of a problem, but only recognize it. He states that Scientology could, along with Reich's theories, form a new form of therapy that could supplant psychiatry, although "any organizational dogma" would first need to be removed. Burroughs also talks at length about the E-meter, demonstrating his considerable knowledge of its workings and a grasp of the associated jargon.

Then bad news came from two old friends. Antony Balch had been diagnosed with inoperable stomach cancer, and Brion Gysin had colon cancer, which surgery removed, but effectively ended his sex life, sending him spiraling into even worse degrees of paranoia. Balch had been in poor health for more than a year, and Burroughs had put it down as hypochondria, telling him to "take up karate and fight it off."

In May, 1975, Burroughs was offered the chance to teach at the Jack Kerouac School of Disembodied Poetics at the Naropa Institute, in Boulder, Colorado. Burroughs enjoyed teaching there in the relaxed atmosphere, but wondered about the man who had established the school, Chogyam Trungpa Rinpoche, who drank a lot and had a tendency towards violence. Burroughs had been reluctant to delve into Buddhism like many of his writer friends, although he had dabbled in it and found it mildly interesting. He thought that it turned good writers bad, for one thing. Still, in November he signed up for a two week retreat in a hut in Vermont owned by Trungpa. He enjoyed the solitude, but left no more of a Buddhist than when he arrived. Two years later, he wrote about his experiences with Trungpa and suggested that Buddhism was not compatible with writing, but that it might provide something to write about later on. "I even got copy out of Scientology," he quipped. In this essay, he makes reference to exteriorization and silence, and repeats his phrase: "Maya am I?" – which fused his dual interests of the Mayans and Scientology. He also made reference to Korzybski and Castañeda, tying together his interests from across throughout his life.

When he returned to New York he moved into an old Y.M.C.A building on Bowery Street, which became known as "the Bunker," due to a complete absence of sunlight within the building. Once again, he enjoyed the peace and quiet. At the Bunker Burroughs of course had his own orgone accumulator installed, and a range of weapons (purchased mail-order from the sort of adverts about which he wrote "Personal Magnetism"). Soon Grauerholz moved in with him.

On February 6th, 1976, Burroughs' sixty-second birthday, he received a telegram from Ian Sommerville: "HAPPY BIRTHDAY. LOTS OF LOVE. LOTS OF PROMISE NO REALIZATION." A few hours later he received another telegram, this time from Balch: "IAN SOMMERVILLE KILLED IN CAR ACCIDENT FEBRUARY 5. FUNERAL FEBRUARY 12, BATH." Sommerville had been driving home from the post office after sending his birthday telegram, when his car hit another vehicle. The accident was not Sommerville's fault, as the other driver had made an incorrect signal. To Burroughs, the cause of his death, however, was something entirely different. Not long before the accident, Gysin had passed along some bad news to Sommerville. Sommerville had recently slept with a woman for the first time, and the woman's boyfriend was the editor of a magazine called *The Fanatic*. By way of revenge, he published a profile of Sommerville that included, among other things, a depiction of his penis, graphic details about his sex life, and unflattering out-of-context quotes about and by Burroughs. Burroughs was furious with Billy Levy, the editor. It was his opinion that the article was intended to kill Sommerville, like a curse of sorts

Burroughs had known Sommerville for seventeen years, almost half of the man's life. His death was an awful blow, and Burroughs, who was off junk, took to drinking heavily. He attempted to contact Sommerville via séances, and consulted a Tibetan lama called Dudjom Rinpoch, who told him that Sommerville was stuck in a level of hell, unable to be reborn.

In the summer, more trouble began when Billy was invited to Naropa by Ginsberg, and given a job as a teaching assistant. His alcoholism was at its worst, and in July he was hospitalized after vomiting blood, and diagnosed with cirrhosis of the liver. In August it happened again, and he was taken to Denver General Hospital, where, by chance, there was the only team of surgeons in the world capable of performing a liver transplant. Billy was in a coma for more than a week before receiving the liver of a young woman who had died of a stroke. When someone wanted read to him, Burroughs was furious: "Dammit! Don't read that thing to him, he's in a fucking coma and he might listen." He was thinking of Hubbard, of course, who once said, "Speech or sound in the vicinity of an 'unconscious' person should be punished criminally," because of the engrams it creates.

One might say it was an amazing stroke of luck that led Billy to receive the liver, as anywhere else in the world he would have died, but for Billy it was a curse. He didn't ask for the new liver, and he didn't want it. He lived for another five years, in pain and constantly depressed. For the first few years, Burroughs visited

196

his son often, although Billy showed a great deal of hostility to his father. He was miserable, in and out of hospital for infections and problems related to his transplant, and he never gave up drinking. He was intent on dying, and no one could stop him. Burroughs stayed with Billy as much as possible, but after a few years it was obvious to him that there was nothing he could do, and his visits became less frequent. Burroughs even had his son institutionalized at the Denver Psychiatric Hospital, despite his own experiences and beliefs. When he was released not much had changed. Billy was killing himself, and on March 3rd, 1981, he succeeded.

Besides the hopelessness of the situation, one other reason that kept Burroughs from travelling to Colorado to be with Billy in the final years was that Burroughs had gotten hooked on heroin again. In New York he was an icon of the punk scene, and his home at the Bunker put him in close proximity with a lot of drugs. Grauerholz's influence had kept him clean, but when he took off for a break in Kansas, Burroughs slipped back into the habit. One visitor recalled him staring at a wall, saying, "Nothing comes out of the clear blue sky. You've got your memory track, everything you've seen and heard." Again, this is a reference to Scientology. "Memory track" is a term used to describe a consciousness going back through time, in different bodies. For Burroughs, though, he had severed the conscious connection to Scientology and claimed that it was a "Buddhist thing." He also talked about the subconscious mind and how it can be triggered, which shows the influence of the reactive mind on his outlook, while once again he appears reluctant to connect it with the dogma of Scientology.

In 1977 Burroughs was again nearly brought to the silver screen, this time by Jacques Stern, who reappeared after a long absence, and was as weird as ever. He paid Burroughs $20,000 for a year's option on *Junky*, but the project was a disaster, of course, with Burroughs finally coming to appreciate just how much of a crackpot his old friend was. Terry Southern and Dennis Hopper were brought into the project, but it quickly fell apart.

The following year *The Third Mind* was released. Written

by Burroughs and Gysin, it can be seen as a history and demonstration of, as well as a guide to, the Cut-up Method. They had worked intermittently on the text-illustration project for more than a decade, but had been unable to find a publisher due to the expense of printing. In the book, they explain that the project had begun in 1965, and was inspired by a self-help guide called *Think and Grow Rich*, which stated that when two minds come together, a third is created. Burroughs and Gysin had long held that their collaboration and their friendship produced such a third mind.

In December of that year was the Nova Convention. It was envisioned as an "homage to Burroughs" that would consist of a number of lectures and seminars between academics from Europe and North America, with performances by Keith Richards and Patti Smith (although Richards was forced to drop out due to a heroin bust). The event was a landmark recognition of Burroughs' influence on contemporary culture.

Burroughs' next book was *Cities of the Red Night*, the first in a trilogy of surprisingly comprehensible novels. Published in 1981, *Cities* features a relatively straightforward (by Burroughs' standard, at least) plot, and whilst it is far-reaching in terms of space and time, it is fairly easy to read, unlike his earlier work. The novel took him nearly seven years to write, because of a number of problems in his life, and partly because he was hit by a nasty bout of writer's block, and unable to produce much of anything for a whole year. In the end, Grauerholz was saddled with the task of editing the book "into present time," which involved extensive changes.

The book is comprised of the three styles of writing that most appealed to Burroughs throughout his life – boy's adventure stories, detective fiction, and sci-fi. There are references to Reich and Castañeda, to Egyptian, Mayan, and Aztec hieroglyphics, and several to Hassan ibn Sabbah and the number 23. Most notably there is Virus B-23, "the virus of biological mutation... this agent occasioned biologic alterations in those affected— fatal in many cases, permanent and hereditary in the survivors, who became carriers of the strain." This is a reference to the "aberrations" described by Hubbard in *Dianetics* – in other words, the engrams that predispose humans to a great many flaws and issues to which clears are immune. In Burroughs' version, the aberrations cause sexual frenzies and death. There are a few subtle jokes that acknowledge Burroughs' inspiration for Virus B-23. His version of the virus has it turning Europeans from black to white (Burroughs suspected Hubbard of racism, due to his use of "wog"), he makes a quip that the virus "might quiet the uh silent majority" (a nod to the idea that silence would prevent new engrams from being created), and jokes that the virus might possibly be dealt with in "past time" (for Scientology processing to work, a preclear must be in present time).

There is also mention of Academy 23, which was one of the names Burroughs proposed for the training schools that he considered opening. In *Cities*, Academy 23 is where one of the Chinese characters, Yen Lee, was trained:

> "Unlike his counterparts in western countries, he had been carefully selected for a high level of intuitive adjustment, and trained accordingly to imagine and explore seemingly fantastic potentials in any situation, while at the same time giving equal consideration to prosaic and practical aspects. He had developed an attitude at once probing and impersonal, remote and alert. He did not know when the training had begun, since in Academy 23 it was carried out in a context of reality."

While Burroughs' ideas for an academy included Scientology, what he is describing here appears to actually *be* Scientology. Lee sounds like a trained auditor, particularly with the description, "probing and impersonal, remote and alert."

People from Burroughs' past make walk-on appearances throughout the book. There's Kiki, the boy from Tangier, and Bernabé Jurado, his Mexican attorney. The book visits Central and South America, as well as New York and Tangier, and there's even a reference to Pharr – the little town where he'd first set up as a farmer in Texas.

In the late seventies and early eighties, Burroughs was lecturing regularly, and in his talks we can see some of the ideas from *Cities*, and his next two novels, *The Place of Dead Roads* and *The Western Lands*. Burroughs at this stage is still interested in telepathy, claiming most human communication is telepathic, and that telepathy is possible between species and even life on different planets. He states in lectures that he believes in reincarnation ("I more or less take that for granted"), the power of wishing machines, and still holds onto Reich's orgone theory. Burroughs was a popular speaker, but now and then hecklers would observe that many of his statements were either patently untrue, or mere conjecture based upon little evidence. In one case, he tried to explain to his audience that a person would die if they could not dream, and when asked for proof of this, he stumbled along just claiming that he knew it because he had heard it somewhere. Of course, Burroughs had never needed much in the way of evidence to believe in something, but he believed he had a scientific mind, and would attempt to speak of the scientific values of his interests. The crowds, however, came to see a show and Burroughs invariably delivered, making his dubious statements with perfect droll delivery, and always got a positive response.

The wishing machine was something Burroughs really did take seriously. It was, after all, working on the same principals as a curse, and in fact one didn't even need a wishing machine, he explained, as it was merely symbolic. He claimed to have learned about it in a book whose title would no doubt have excited Burroughs – *On the Frontiers of Science: Strange Machines You Can Build* – although he also said that he read the original article, which was published in 1956.[20]

His interests in his final years appear increasingly on the fringes of science. He was interested in incubi and succubi, as detailed in

20 The wishing machine in question was promoted heavily in *Astounding Science Fiction* by the magazine's editor, John W. Campbell Jnr. Campbell was also a big supporter of Hubbard's Dianetics theory, and published his breakthrough article in the magazine.

Victor Bokris' *Reports from the Bunker*, and it was not much of a leap for Burroughs, whose visions of space travel involved "the astral or dream body" (much like thetans) released from their human prison. In his essay, "Civilian Defense," he references Aleister Crowley in calling these spirits a "body of light." He became more interested in Crowley and his understandings of astral travel, which bear remarkable similarities to Hubbard's process of exteriorization, and were in fact most likely the inspiration for Hubbard's own theories. Burroughs painted a portrait of Crowley in 1988 and claimed to still have an interest in him a year before his death, in 1996. [21]

After the publication of *Cities of the Red Night* and Billy's death, Burroughs joined Grauerholz in Lawrence, Kansas, for a short break. He was as surprised as anyone to find that he actually enjoyed the place. When he returned to New York, he found that his landlord was threatening to double his rent, and that strengthened his resolve: he was moving to Kansas. Burroughs had enjoyed himself in New York, a city of which he was always fond, but it had taken its toll on his health and, in 1981, he was a senior citizen in search of a place to see out his remaining days. It was, he told Gysin, "a nice spot for old age."

In Kansas, Burroughs first rented a place, and then purchased a small house on Leonard Avenue. On a shelf sat a human skull, and there was an eclectic mix of reading material, from weaponry magazines to books about cats. Grauerholz and other friends drove him to the methadone clinic and cooked his breakfast. He took over office space in the downtown area that used to be occupied by a law firm, and set up his headquarters. Together with Grauerholz, he assembled an efficient system for keeping up with the business of being an internationally renowned author.

---

21 Burroughs was well aware of the connection between Hubbard and Crowley. Hubbard had lived with and participated in experiments in black magic with one of Crowley's associates, Jack Parsons, not long before writing "Dianetics," and in a 1952 lecture, Hubbard recommended a book by Crowley, referring to him as "my very good friend." Many of the ideas in Dianetics are similar (and probably borrowed from) Crowley's teachings, including astral travel/exteriorization, Magical Memory/Reactive Mind, a hatred of psychiatry, and the process of mocking up. Their respective organizations even had similar logos.

In Lawrence he took in a cat he called Ruski, and then began taking in strays. The man who'd once brutalized these animals as a young junky was now a cat-loving senior. Over his final years he had many cats, in in them he saw his old friends. In Ruski he found a psychic connection to Kiki. The cat, he observed, had many of the same habits. He developed the same intense attachment to these animals that he had with the people in his life whom he had loved. They came to change his life, and in 1984 he wrote in his journal, "My relationship with my cats has saved me from a deadly, pervasive ignorance." When confronted with the possibility of nuclear war, he said, "I'll go heavily armed to the supermarket and shoot my way to the cat-food counter."

Although Burroughs had maintained an interest in guns since his time at Los Alamos, it was in Kansas that it truly became a passion. Despite once saying, "I'm not a collector," he had an admirable collection of weapons, and now that he was no longer a city-dweller, he had the space to use them. In his Nova Trilogy, Burroughs wrote about the weapons necessary to fight invisible control mechanisms, but in his Red Night Trilogy the weapons of choice were the kind that put holes in heads. "It's really concerned with weaponry more than anything else," he explained. "Weaponry on all levels."

Another of Burroughs' preoccupations during this period, and one which became a central theme of *The Place of Dead Roads*, was time travel. "Time travel is something all of us do," he said. "You just have to think about what you were doing an hour ago and you're there." What Burroughs is describing is Hubbard's notion of recall. Hubbard said

> "A person can 'send' a portion of his mind to a past period on either a mental or combined mental and physical basis and can re-experience incidents which have taken place in his past in the same fashion and with the same sensations as before."

This was time travel, in Burroughs' mind, and that's what he meant in the book's title – "dead roads" are people and places from your past that you can revisit.

> "Remember a red brick house on Jane Street?
> Your breath quickens as you mount the worn,
> red-carpeted stairs… The road to 4 Calle Larachi,
> Tangier, or 24 Arrundle Terrace in London. So
> many dead roads you will never use again…"

Burroughs maintained that space travel was also possible, but that man had become limited in his attempts. To escape the confines of this planet, "planet Earth, place of dead roads, dead purposes," one needed more than NASA was attempting. He explained in interviews and lectures in the early eighties his notion of space travel. Sending men into space in capsules that cost millions of dollars was, to Burroughs, absurd. He knew better. Scientology taught the techniques of exteriorization. A man's thetan could travel between planets, so why even bother with the body? It was just another dead road.

In *Dead Roads*, Burroughs's alter ego, Kim, thinks about space travel as his "only purpose," and a means of escape. He considers the necessities for leaving this planet – namely a change in biological form in order to adapt to the environment of space. And what is the environment of space? "SILENCE." Humans need to evolve in order to deal with silence. It was from Scientology that Burroughs took the idea that silence is important, a method of avoiding triggering an engram.

Harkening back to *The Soft Machine*, Burroughs introduces the idea of "prerecordings" that control our actions. "The only thing prerecorded in a prerecorded universe is the prerecordings themselves: the film. The unforgivable sin is to tamper with the prerecordings." Of course, this plays off the notion of a reactive mind and engrams which can be triggered by predetermined stimuli.

The Place of Dead Roads was published in 1983, when Burroughs was nearly seventy. As always there were hundreds of pages of leftover material, and these were used to begin work on the next book, the final installment in the trilogy – *The Western Lands*. Referring to the West Bank of the Nile, which the ancient Egyptians considered the Land of the Dead, this book deals with life after death, in addition to the themes of time and space travel. "I never doubted the possibility of an afterlife, nor the existence of gods," he later said.[22] Indeed, even as a child, Burroughs had argued with his atheist father over such things.

In 1982, Burroughs wrote "I consider that immortality is the only goal worth striving for: immortality in Space." His view was that time was finite but space was infinite, but that humans could work to free themselves of their bodies (exteriorization) and adapt to the conditions of space (silence, thereby erasing the reactive mind), and could thereby become immortal. This was Burroughs' interpretation, more than twenty years after reading *Dianetics*, of Hubbard's identification of man's primary goal as survival. Although he no longer identified in any way as a Scientologist, the religion's basic tenants had become a firm part of his worldview.

In *The Western Lands*, finished in 1986 and published the following year, William Seward Hall (based upon Burroughs himself) is killed, and attempts to "write his way out of death." Characters from his life and work fade away, and at the end even the narrator signs off "because he had reached the end of words." Reviewers took this as a sign that Burroughs was done with writing, and although this was not his final novel, he did little writing in his remaining years, mostly just waking in the night to jot down sketches from his dreams.

Since 1959, with help from Brion Gysin, Burroughs had experimented with visual art. With Gysin's death in 1986, he took up art as more serious pursuit. Previously he had felt awkward about moving in on his friend's territory, but now he was able to explore a new sort of cut-up – shotgun art. "Using a shotgun blast to hit the pressurized spray paint is just an extension of the random principal since it's practically impossible to foresee for yourself what will happen." He was sure that he could see

22 Compare this with the character of Kim Carsons in *The Place of Dead Roads*: "Kim has never doubted the possibility of an afterlife or the existence of gods."

portraits in the resulting patterns. In 1989, in an attempt to avoid the criticism of his art as frivolous, he wrote formal statement that can be applied to his visual art and also his written work. In it he cites Castañeda, prerecordings, magic, and possession.

> "In the Carlos Castañeda books, Don Juan makes a distinction between the tonal universe and the nagual. The tonal universe is the everyday cause-and-effect universe, which is predictable because it is pre-recorded. The nagual is the unknown, the unpredictable, the uncontrollable. For the nagual to gain access, the door of chance must be open. There must be a random factor."

In a 1986 radio interview that was never broadcast, Burroughs' interviewer asked him about his interest in what lay in "the juncture between science and mystery," citing Scientology, Reich, and Castañeda. Burroughs called it a "life-long preoccupation," and cited childhood experiences with science fiction novels. In the eighties, Burroughs was again heavily into science fiction, and his interest in the bizarre had not abated. He also talked about telepathy and time travel, which he considered absolutely a part of reality, even if science couldn't be bothered to prove them true.

Entering his final decade, Burroughs was still fascinated with the bizarre and the wonderful, and kept up to date with the world through his various magazine subscriptions and books about fringe science. Yet he had mellowed greatly, and although he retained some of his ideas, he was keen to draw a line between his present self and his past self. In 1990 he claimed, "I probably wouldn't stand by many of the things I said 20 years ago." He appeared tired of questions about, for example, quotes from *The Job*. He was now an old man whose primary interest in life was his cats, not revolution.

In 1992, forty-one years after the Ugly Spirit had made its appearance with the death of his wife, Burroughs undertook an exorcism in an attempt to free himself of possession. It had plagued him all this time, causing him untold hurt. Psychiatry had failed to cure him, Scientology had failed, everything he tried failed to remove the stubborn demon inside him. But this was no Christian exorcism. He disdained organized religion, especially Christianity in the American Bible Belt, the inhabitants of which he called the "Moron Majority."[23] Conducted by a Navajo shaman, the ceremony was intense, and Burroughs felt freed. When the shaman later described the spirit, Burroughs claimed to have seen it in his paintings.

In his final years, Burroughs appeared to think a great deal about Scientology, although he had absolutely nothing positive to say. A year before his death, he was interviewed by *LA Weekly*, who asked him if he was still interested in in the religion. He was quick to dismiss the suggestion:

"Oh no, no. I left Scientology way back. It had some ideas, but Hubbard just cribbed these ideas from everywhere. He stole and cursed the source. He's dead now."

Throughout his life, Burroughs wrote down his dreams, and in his journals from the last years, which also contain his thoughts and ideas, he occasionally made reference to Hubbard, sometimes hateful and always mocking. In his last published book, *My Education: A Book of Dreams*, he wrote,

"A feeling of dread... Met L. Ron Hubbard. In an empty room with the lathes and plaster showing, somehow evoking a derelict dance studio. He has a dead white face and a white suit of some wickerlike material.
"'I have looked forward to meeting you for a long time.'"

---

23 In interviews throughout the seventies and eighties, Burroughs demonstrated an increasing intolerance for religion. He proudly proclaims himself "anti-Christian," and calls Protestantism "the most virulent spiritual poison."

This was written a few years after Hubbard died. He also dreamed about being at a Scientology center with Ian Sommerville. Later, he mocked Hubbard, picking on the supposed quote that he examined in his essay, "Immortality":

> "L. Ron Hubbard, the founder of Scientology, says that the secret of life has been discovered... by *him*. The secret of life is *to survive*. The rightest right a man could be is to live infinitely long. And I venture to suggest that the wrongest wrong a man could be might well be the means whereby such relative immortality was obtained. To survive what, exactly? Enemy attack, what else? We have now come full circle, from nineteenth-century crude literalism through behaviorism, the conditioned reflex, back to the magical universe, where nothing happens unless some force, being, or power wills it to happen."

In November, 1996, he wrote, "L. Ron Hubbard needs a knife in his gizzard," and in January he made fun of Hubbard's incorporation of science fiction into Scientology and his time at sea:

> "L. Ron Hubbard appears in a dream, his face with a deep space tan. We will head a streamlined Scientology takeover. He is dressed in what looks like deep-sea-fishing, certainly nautical garb.
> "Well, why not give it a glim? Recall he was human, then he wasn't:
> "'I am not from this planet, but I got the best intentions.'"

Later, he mocked the government for making laws that criminalize states of being, such as being addicted to a drug. "L. Ron Hubbard called them 'suppressive persons.' He was one himself. Always accuse others of doing what you are doing."

He even appeared to finally rid himself of his interest in auditing, repeating an idea that had troubled him since before his time at Saint Hill – that engrams don't just leave you, they are passed on to someone else.

> "What the hell is auditing? Listening to trauma *and passing it on.*
> "Here is one revolting process: look at someone on the street, and imagine everything that is wrong with *you* is *wrong with him or her.*
> "(Unburden that whole load of shit on some passerby. May encounter a tough one, catches on straightaway and throws it back with intent and interest.)
> …
> "(There is no doubt about it: Scientology is evil and basically ill-intentioned and nasty.)"

Around two months prior to his death, Burroughs reminisced about all the methods he'd tried in search of an answer, and questioned just what it was that he was really looking for the whole time:

> "Do I want to know? I have tried psychoanalysis, yoga, Alexander's posture method, done a seminar with Robert Monroe (the *Journeys out of the Body* man), EST in London, Scientology, Sweat Lodges and *a yuwipi* ceremony.
> "Looking for the answer?
> "Why? Do you want to know *the secret?*
> "Hell, no. Just what I need to know, to do what I can do."

Burroughs had softened a great deal in his final years, indicating that somehow he had found what he was looking for. Through a long life of searching and experimenting, he had found peace. In May, 1996, Timothy Leary passed away. Burroughs spoke to him on the phone just hours before his death, and told his old friend that he loved him. This was a long way from the man who considered love a female-created virus. He said that Leary was not afraid of death because he believed in an afterlife, a view he shared. Over the following year Herbert Huncke, Terry Southern, and Allen Ginsberg all passed away. He'd outlived all of his old friends, and now even his cats were dying off. The last to go was his favorite, Fletch, who passed away on July 9th. A few weeks later, on August 2nd, 1997, it was Burroughs' turn. His final journal entry perhaps explains why he had mellowed so much in old age, and why he had finally found peace: "The only thing can resolve conflict is love, like I felt for Fletch… Love. What is it? Most natural painkiller what there is. LOVE."

Notes

Chapter One

Biographical details about his childhood are from Ted Morgan's *Literary Outlaw: The Life and Times of William S. Burroughs.* Most of the details from his time as a farmer in Texas until he moves to Tangier are from *The Letters of William S. Burroughs: 1945-1959*, edited by Oliver Harris. The remaining details are a mixture of *Letters* and *Outlaw*. Additional sources are listed below, or stated in the text.

"Ivy never..." – *Last Words: The Final Journals of William S. Burroughs*, edited by James Grauerholz

Later opinion of Ivy and choice of William Lee pseudonym – *William S. Burroughs*, by Jennie Skerl

Last visit to church at six years old – 1978 interview with Gerard-George Lamaire, in *Burroughs Live: The Collected Interviews of William S. Burroughs*, edited by Sylvère Lotringer

"Sweet dreams" and dream/opiates connection – from the preface to *Junky*, by William S. Burroughs: "Actually my earliest memories are coloured by a fear of nightmares. I was afraid to be alone, and afraid of the dark, and afraid to go to sleep because of dreams where a supernatural horror seemed always on the point of taking shape. I was afraid some day the dream would still be there when I woke up. I recall hearing a maid talk about opium and how smoking opium brings sweet dreams, and I said: 'I will smoke opium when I grow up.'"

"As a young child…" – from the biographical essay, "The Name is Burroughs," in *The Adding Machine*, by William S. Burroughs

Harvard marijuana use – 1978 interview with Richard Goldstein, in *Burroughs Live*

Start of jiu-jitsu training – preface to *Junky*

Visit to the Egyptology Department in Chicago and subsequent speculation on nature of viruses and possession – from introduction to *Queer*, by William S. Burroughs

Reading Chandler and Hammett – *Word Virus*, edited by James Grauerholz

"Gangsterling" – *Word Virus*

"my Old lady…" – *Naked Lunch*, by William S. Burroughs

Telepathic games – according to eyewitnesses mentioned in *Word Virus*

Kerouac's false claims re: the orgone accumulator – Burroughs explains in the his essay, "My Experiences with Wilhelm Reich's Orgone Box" in *The Adding Machine*, that Kerouac was repeating and elaborating incorrectly upon information he had likely obtained from Neal Cassady, who did visit Burroughs in Pharr, and did witness the orgone accumulator.

Burroughs studying Mayans in Texas – Grauerholz's editorial comments in *Word Virus*

Additional information regarding his views on Mayans/Aztecs – Paul H. Wild's essay, "William S. Burroughs and the Maya gods of death: the uses of archaeology" in *College*

Literature, Winter 2008

"in some crime magazine..." Allen Ginsberg interviewed by Ruas in 1975, in *Burroughs Live*

"He is such a child..." – *Queer*

"Schlupping" – *I Celebrate Myself: The Somewhat Private Life of Allen Ginsberg*, by Bill Morgan. This phrase was also used by Burroughs in *Naked Lunch*.

"steep himself in vice" – *"William Burroughs: An Essay,"* by Alan Ansen

Jacques Stern as a Scientologist – Burroughs mentions his beliefs in *Rub Out the Words: The Letters of William S. Burroughs 1959-1974*, edited by Bill Morgan, calling him "Reverend Stern" as he was training to become a Scientology auditor in 1960. In *Beat Hotel: Ginsberg, Burroughs, and Corso in Paris, 1957-1963*, Barry Miles claims that Stern helped Gysin in pushing Burroughs into Scientology.

"trailed long vines..." – *Nothing is True; Everything is Permitted*, by John Geiger

Gysin's incorrect views on Hassan ibn Sabbah – "Under the Influence of William S. Burroughs" by Nikolas Schreck, in *Beatdom #10*

""They produced a certain..." – Gysin paraphrasing Burroughs in an interview with Terry Wilson in *Here to Go: Planet R-101*

"Retreat 23" inference – "St. Louis Return" in *Word Virus*

Chapter Two

All of Burroughs' letters from this section of the book are taken from *Rub Out the Words*, unless otherwise stated. General biographical details from *Literary Outlaw* and also *Rub Out the Words*.

The false version of account – *Lee Konstantinou's essay, "William S. Burroughs's Wild Ride with Scientology." Essay available from various websites, including http://*

io9.com/5800673/william-s-burroughss-wild-ride-with-scientology

Gysin and the Cookes – information from interviews in *Here to Go*, *The Process*, by Brion Gysin, and *Nothing is True; Everything is Permitted.*

Burroughs blaming Gysin for Scientology introduction - "William S. Burroughs, Charles Gatewood, and Sidetripping" by Charles Gatewood on RealityStudio.org.

"was never involved" – Gysin interviewed in *Naked Lens: Beat Cinema*, by Jack Sargeant

Details about Scientology – taken from Hubbard's *Dianetics*, as this was the text Burroughs originally studied

Influence of Korzybski and others on Hubbard – "Possible origins for Dianetics and Scientology" by Jon Atack and "General Semantics vs. Scientology" by José Klingbeil

Burroughs' 1939 attempts to think in terms of pictures – *Literary Outlaw*

"In fact, the cut-ups..." – Ginsberg interviewed in the *International Tines*, issue 148

"Ian says Bill is only..." – *Beat Hotel*

"automatic writing" – *Letters*

"word hoard" – *Word Virus*

"Use of cut ups..." – *Rub Out the Word*

Auditing sheets – New York Public Library Berg Collection

"In Naked Lunch..." – 1964 interview with Eric Mottram in *Burroughs Live*

"To concern yourself..." – 1961 interview with Corso and Ginsberg in *Burroughs Live*

Second lowest BBC ratings – *Back in No Time: The Brion Gysin Reader*, edited by Jason Weiss

Scientology cut-up – Berg Collection

Burroughs taking Scientology classes – although these classes are not mentioned in his letters, Brion Gysin claimed in *Naked Lens* that Burroughs was attending Scientology classes throughout 1962

"Security Checking Fundamentals" – Berg Collection

Information about Scientologese and connection between

language and mind control – Robert Kaufman's *Inside Scientology: How I Joined Scientology and Became Superhuman* and Margery Wakefield's *Understanding Scientology: The Demon Cult*. Also see a number of ex-Scientologist forums online for information pertaining to linguistics and difficulty leaving the religion.

Burroughs' quotes from the Edinburgh Festival – published in *Transatlantic Review #11* (some parts also included in *The Third Mind*, by Burroughs and Gysin, and *Word Virus*)

Letters to Balch – some included in *Rub Out the Word*, others published on RealityStudio.org

It was Gysin's idea to use Scientology materials in The Cut Ups – *Naked Lens*

"When Huxley got Buddhism..." – *The Retreat Diaries*, by William S. Burroughs

"Cut Up with Scientology lit" – Berg Collection

"E Meter Errors – Comm Cycle Error" – Berg Collection

"madness is confusion..." – *Letters*

"Auditing and Comm Cycles" – Berg Collection

"Repetitive Rudiments" – Berg Collection

"Auditing and Assessment" – Berg Collection

"Study" – Berg Collection

"clearest statement" – 1970 interview with Allen Ginsberg in *Burroughs Live*

"Heaven and hell exist..." 1964 interview with Eric Mottram in *Burroughs Live*

Sommerville's dislike of Hubbard and Hubbard's alleged use of tape recorders – *Rub Out the Words*

Details about Masterton and *Mayfair* – 2012 interview with the author

Chapter Three

Most of the details regarding Burroughs' time at Saint Hill come from materials in the New York Public Library's Berg Collection. Additional details mentioned below.

Saint Hill brochure – Berg Collection

Early experiences at Saint Hill – *Literary Outlaw* and *Rub Out the Words*

Gysin joking about Burroughs making money from Scientology – he is quoted in Barry Miles' *El Hombre Invisible* as saying, "[Burroughs] must be one of the few people who has made more money from them than they made from him."

Sec Check questions – *Literary Outlaw*

Joberg – Berg Collection, *Ali's Smile: Naked Scientology*, by William S. Burroughs

Cut-ups – Berg Collection

Clearing Course info – *Rub Out the Words*

Other claims – Burroughs wrote in various letters that he would continue to study Scientology

"Scientology was useful…" – quoted in *El Hombre Invisible*

"New Dimensions in Writing" – courtesy of Michael Butterworth

Masterton quote – 2012 interview with the author

"Fantastically successful…" – *Rub Out the Words*

Democratic convention and Kerouac meeting – *Literary Outlaw*

Sept. 10, 1968 letter to Balch – hosted on RealityStudio.org

Interested in sickness caused by Clearing Course materials – Burroughs had underlined passages in Scientology literature relating to claims by L. Ron Hubbard that "criminal types" who had stolen upper level training materials were unable to successfully use them, and instead became very ill.

"Clearing course materials only…" – *Rub Out the Words*

"Love" and "hate" tattoos on Culverwell's knuckles – reported by J.G. Ballard in his Burroughs obituary, with further discussion in an essay called "William S. Burroughs and J.G. Ballard" on RealityStudio.org

"rolling around with…" and subsequent letters – *Rub Out the Words* "the reactive mind mirrors…" – *Rub Out the Words*

Chapter Four

HCO letter of treason – Berg Collection
Letter to Bill Flemming – *Rub Out the Words*
"Having been giving…" – *Rub Out the Words*
"flattening an item…" – *Rub Out the Words*
Correspondence with Cooke – *Rub Out the Words*
"there was too much" – 1972 interview with Robert Palmer in *Burroughs Live*
Clearing course materials as the format of *The Wild Boys* – *Rub Out the Words*: "I have found a format for *the wild boy* book … The *clearing course material* worked out very well as a framework since it is in fact a book of the dead"
"…film glimpses will occur…" – from Burroughs' review of Robert Kaufman's *Inside Scientology* in *Naked Scientology*
Interest in silence – 1978 interview with Richard Goldstein in *Burroughs Live*
Cutting out the Times article – Berg Collection
M.O.B – Berg Collection, *Rub Out the Words*
Dream Calendar – *El Hombre Invisible*
Dream of Hubbard – Berg Collection
"Arc of the Three Engrams" essay/fiction – Berg Collection
Letters after publication in *The Rat* – *Rub Out the Words*
Visit by Gaiman – *Rub Out the Words*
Unpublished essay – Berg Collection
"aberrative thinking" interview – with *AM/PA* magazine, in *Burroughs Live*
Letter to Mr. Harr – *Rub Out the Words*
"Standard Dianetic Gains" – Berg Collection
Creation of Ah Pook is Here – *Observed While Falling*, by Malcolm McNeill, and 2007 interview with McNeill at http://www.vlib.us/beats/malcolmmcneill.html. Richard Goodman also recalled McMaster talking about

Notes

Scientology at Burroughs flat: http://ducts.org/09_00/profiles/profiles_burroughs.html

Mother's death – *Literary Outlaw*

Newspaper clippings – Berg Collection

Dream about Hubbard – Berg Collection

"Every time…" – Masterton 2012 interview with the author

Making Naked Lunch a movie – *Literary Outlaw*, *Rub Out the Words*

Angry letter – Berg Collection

Ali's Smile etc. publication details – *Collecting William S. Burroughs in Print*, by Eric C. Shoaf

Switzerland, Los Angeles, and London – *Literary Outlaw*, *Rub Out the Words*

Xenu – *The Road to Xenu: A Narrative Account of Life in Scientology*, by Margery Wakefield, *Scientology*, edited by James R. Lewis

Correspondence with Cooke – *Rub Out the Words*

Using recordings against Moka Bar, Scientology – *El Hombre Invisible* (quote "I have frequently observed…" originally from *The Job*.

"Brion's a prankster…" – "William S. Burroughs, Charles Gatewood, and Sidetripping" by Charles Gatewood on RealityStudio.org

Events surrounding publication of *Inside Scientology* – foreword to *Inside Scientology*

Correspondence with Girodias – *Rub Out the Words*

Early draft of the review – Berg Collection

Interest in McManaway – *Literary Outlaw*

Biographical details – *Literary Outlaw*, *Word Virus*, *Rub Out the Words*

"Maybe I'm as crazy…" – *Literary Outlaw*

"take up karate…" – *Rub Out the Words*

Essay about Trungpa – "Obeying Chogyam Trungpa" from 1977 *CoEvolution Quarterly*, accessed online at http://www.wholeearth.com/issue/2013/article/372/obeying.chogyam.trungpa

Sommerville's death and Billy's medical problems – *Literary*

Outlaw

""Nothing comes out..." – *With William Burroughs: A Report from the Bunker*, by Victor Bokris

The technology of wishing – June 25, 1986, from the Naropa Poetics Audio Archive

"a nice spot..." – quoted in *Literary Outlaw*

Cats – *The Cat Inside*

"I'll go heavily armed..." – 1987 interview with James Fox in *Burroughs Live*

"It's really concerned..." – 1982 interview with Chris Bohn in *Burroughs Live*

"Time travel is something..." – quoted in *El Hombre Invisible*

"A person can 'send'..." – *Dianetics*

"I never doubted..." – 1982 interview with Duncan Fallowell in *Burroughs Live*

"I considered that..." – quoted in *El Hombre Invisible*, similar quotations also appear throughout interviews

"Using a shotgun..." – quoted in *El Hombre Invisible*

"I probably wouldn't..." – 1990 interview with Kristine McKenna in *Burroughs Live*

Acknowledgments

A special thanks goes to my wife, Amy, without whom this book would not have been possible. Thanks also to Michael Hendrick, the good people at the New York Public Library, Matthew Levi Stevens, Spencer Kansa, Keith Seward, Charles Gatewood, Graham Masterton, and Michael Butterworth. This book also owes a debt of gratitude to the Ubuweb and Reality Studio websites.

14118860R00125

Printed in Great Britain
by Amazon.co.uk, Ltd.,
Marston Gate.